BRUCE WEBER'S
★ INSIDE ★
BASEBALL
1985

SCHOLASTIC INC.
New York Toronto London Auckland Sydney Tokyo

PHOTO CREDITS

Cover: Chuck Solomon/Focus on Sports. **iv, 6, 10, 32:** New York Yankees. **4, 44:** Kansas City Royals. **7, 13, 14, 30:** Detroit Tigers. **8, 56:** Jay Spencer; Jaybo Photo/Miami. **9, 15, 38:** Baltimore Orioles. **11, 36:** Boston Red Sox. **12, 48:** Chicago White Sox. **16, 76:** Los Angeles Dodgers. **18, 27, 58, 60:** New York Mets. **19, 26, 64:** Chicago Cubs. **20, 62:** Philadelphia Phillies. **21, 66:** St. Louis Cardinals. **22, 72:** San Diego Padres. **23, 74:** Atlanta Braves. **24, 78:** Houston Astros. **25, 68:** Montreal Expos. **28, 50:** California Angels. **34:** Toronto Blue Jays. **40:** Milwaukee Brewers. **42:** Cleveland Indians. **46:** Minnesota Twins. **52:** Seattle Mariners. **54:** Oakland A's. **70:** Pittsburgh Pirates. **80:** San Francisco Giants. **82:** Cincinnati Reds. **84:** Paul H. Roedig/Phillies.

ISBN 0-590-33617-7

12 11 10 9 8 7 6 5 4 3 2 1   3   5 6 7 8 9/8 0/9

Printed in the U.S.A.   01

CONTENTS

Introduction: Who's Next? **1**

American League All-Pro Team **5**

National League All-Pro Team **17**

American League Team Previews **29**

National League Team Previews **59**

Statistics 1984 **85**

   American League Batting **86**

   American League Pitching **93**

   National League Batting **96**

   National League Pitching **103**

Bruce Weber Picks How They'll Finish
   in 1984 **107**

You Pick How They'll Finish
   in 1984 **108**

Yankee first-sacker Don Mattingly hopes
that he won't need another four-hit final
game to win another AL batting tittle.

INTRODUCTION:
Who's Next?

Major-league baseball is rapidly joining basketball in the land of the defeated champion. The National Basketball Association hasn't crowned a repeat champion since 1969, and now it looks as if baseball fans, too, can't wait until the defending champ gets knocked off.

Check the division winners for the past three seasons:

1982: AL — Milwaukee, California;
NL — St. Louis, Atlanta.

1983: AL — Baltimore, Chicago;
NL — Philadelphia, Los Angeles.

1984: AL — Detroit, Kansas City;
NL — Chicago, San Diego.

Not a repeater in the bunch — and that's what makes this game great. If history teaches us any lessons, one should not pick the Tigers, Royals, Cubs, or Padres to lead their respective divisions in '85. But, fools that we may be, we believe that two, possibly three, could well appear in the League Championship Series when they begin on October 8, 1985.

The 1984 season was particularly rewarding because the division champs ended years of frustration for long-suffering fans. The Cubs hadn't won since World War II. The Tigers had gone 16 years without a flag. The Padres had never won. And even the Royals, who had won the AL West as recently as 1980, weren't expected to be in the chase, as late as midseason.

Besides its competitiveness, the other stellar attraction of baseball is its ongoing production of new and exciting stars. All it took to turn on Met fans was the right arm of Dwight Gooden. The teenager blasted National League hitters right out of the batter's box, racking up incredible strike-out totals while challenging the credibility of speed-rating machines.

And in Seattle, where the Mariners make a habit of finishing at the bottom of the standings and lead the league only in firing managers, rookie Mark Langston, up from Chattanooga, was nearly as impressive as Gooden, leading the AL in strikeouts. Combined with rookie first baseman Alvin Davis, the young Mariners gave their fans plenty to cheer about, though the final results only led to the dismissal of another manager.

So let the games of '85 begin. We make no guarantees — save for the fact that the season will be lots of fun. Veterans we've written off will make major comebacks (like Dave Kingman and Joaquin Andujar did last year). Rookies none of us has heard of will make spectacular debuts. (Alvin Davis wasn't even on Seattle's 40-man roster in the winter of 1983–84.) And some brilliant trade or free-agent signing will make one general manager a genius and another an idiot.

Whether your team plays basically at night or mostly during the day, whether it plays indoors or out, whether it plays on plastic grass or the real thing, whether it plays as well as it can (or as well as you think it can), 1985 is bound to be another great year.

— Bruce Weber

Other Kaycee Royals get more publicity, but
gentleman Frank White, their ace second
baseman, does the job day in and day out.

American League
ALL-PRO TEAM

First Base
DON
MATTINGLY
NEW YORK YANKEES

Winning his first AL batting title was easy. Ranking as the league's best first sacker was much more difficult.

But Don Mattingly, who makes things look easy with a bat in his hands, won this race, too. In a league where superstars such as Eddie Murray, Kent Hrbek, and Cecil Cooper play first, Mattingly, at age 23, has risen to the top.

Early last season, Don wasn't even expected to be in the Yankees' starting lineup. It didn't take long, however, for manager Yogi Berra to find a permanent spot for Mattingly and his super-quick bat.

By mid-July, Don and teammate Dave Winfield reached the top of the AL batting charts, and the two battled down to the last day of the season. In the final game, a four-hit performance against the Tigers gave Mattingly a .343 season mark and a three-point win over Winfield. (Winfield won the salary race, out-earning Mattingly by nearly $1.6 million. Mattingly got only $130,000 for his super season.)

Among Don's 207 hits were 44 doubles and 23 homers, which produced 110 RBIs (fifth in the AL). And for a guy who shifted between first base and left and right fields in '83, Don showed Gold Glove potential at first in '84. His future is brilliant.

6

Second Base
LOU
WHITAKER
DETROIT TIGERS

Baseball's outstanding teams have great strength up the middle, particularly in the infield. That's why you have to love the Detroit Tigers. Alan Trammell would be the All-Pro shortstop in any league that did not contain Cal Ripken. And Lou Whitaker has clearly placed himself a cut above the other AL second sackers.

Though Trammell, Kirk Gibson, and a couple of other Tigers made more World Series noise, Whitaker quietly went about being the best in the business all season. A former AL Rookie of the Year (1978), Lou has made a solid contribution year after year, suffering only one off-year (1980, when he slumped to .223 at the plate).

Though not up to his smashing .320 year in 1983, '84 was more satisfying for Lou. The Tigers won it all, of course, and he and pal Trammell were recognized as the AL's top DP pair. The soon-to-be-27-year-old was a major factor in the super-quick Detroit start, hitting .325 in April and knocking in 12 go-ahead and 12 game-winning RBIs. He had the second-highest homer total (13) of his career and even banged his first major-league grand-slammer on September 17.

A gorgeous fielder who's tough around the bag at second, Whitaker should keep his spot as the AL's No. 1 second sacker.

Third Base
BUDDY BELL
TEXAS RANGERS

When the first-ever New York Met team was preparing for its 1962 opener, manager Casey Stengel was asked to name his starting right fielder. Casey, who suffered from occasional memory lapses (as well as dugout snoozes), talked for nearly seven minutes before he finally came up with the answer: "And his name rings a bell. That's his name — Gus Bell."

Gus's son Buddy is somewhat easier to remember — though his Texas teammates played a lot like those crummy Mets of '62.

The phrases *Buddy Bell* and *trading block* often go hand in hand. Rumors fly around Bell's situation every winter. And every spring and summer he's back, doing a first-class job. Where he'll do it in '85 is anyone's guess.

Buddy repeated as the Rangers' leading hitter in '84. But what a difference! A .277 average did it in '83; his 1984 mark was .315, a 38-point improvement. It was also good for fourth in the AL, behind Don Mattingly, Dave Winfield, and Wade Boggs. His 36 doubles were fifth in the league.

These were impressive numbers for the Rangers, who were last in a so-so division. Thus, it would surprise no one if they sent Buddy, good bat and solid glove and all, packing.

Shortstop
CAL RIPKEN
BALTIMORE ORIOLES

Alan Trammell fans may disagree, but Cal Ripken of the Orioles is the once-and-future choice as the AL's top shortstop. He's the best tall-stop, too.

Cal stands a little more than 6–4 and weighs a bit more than 200 pounds. Early critics argued that he was too tall to play shortstop. But his performance in the field and at the plate has silenced everyone.

In his third full season in the big-time, the son of Oriole third-base coach Cal Ripken, Sr., hit a sparkling .304. He was third in the league in hits (195), total bases (327), and extra-base hits (71). He was also among the league leaders in doubles (37) and runs scored (103). No other major-league shortstop matched his 86 RBIs and 27 homers.

He also continued to make progress with his glove. His 583 assists set an AL record for shortstops. He also led the league in putouts (297), chances (904), and DPs (122). Though his .973 fielding percentage was only fifth in the league, 13 of his 23 errors came in one stretch of 32 games.

Thanks to his father's Oriole employment, Ripken has spent most of his life in the Baltimore area. In fact, he buys 25 tickets to every home game for underprivileged kids and senior citizens in his hometown. Cal's a winner off the field, too.

Outfield
DAVE WINFIELD
NEW YORK YANKEES

It took a four-hit final-day performance by Don Mattingly for Dave Winfield to come up just an eyelash short in the 1984 AL batting race. Dave doesn't come up short often, which makes him a sure thing in our All-Pro roster race.

Though his boss, George Steinbrenner, may not totally appreciate him, Dave Winfield is a winner — in and out of the ball park. His charitable acts, through the David M. Winfield Foundation, are well known. (In fact, it's one of the major problems in the Winfield-Steinbrenner miniwar.)

But the fans don't pay serious money to watch a foundation president play baseball. The Winfield they come to see is a total athlete. A superb college basketball player, the 6–6 Winfield could have played in the NBA or NFL had he not chosen to play baseball.

Before last season, Dave was rarely in the batting race. A lifetime .284 hitter, his is a power game. But an early stint on the disabled list put him way behind in the homer race (finishing with 19), and his batting average in May was only .242. Then he went on a tear. By early July, he was hitting .377 and was in his race with Mattingly all the way.

Eighty-five should be fun, too.

Outfield
TONY ARMAS
BOSTON RED SOX

Looking for All-Star outfielders? Check Fenway Park. The Boston Red Sox always seem to be loaded with 'em. And the current trio — Dwight Evans, Jim Rice, and Tony Armas — is as good as any.

Hard to believe that All-Pro Armas "wasted" years in Oakland before being allowed to discover Fenway's friendly confines. It wouldn't surprise anyone if Tony wanted to take the "green monster" in left field home with him for the winter, just to make sure nothing happened to it.

Tony hit everything hard a year ago, which should really come as no surprise. He's always had power. But his 43 homers, eight more than AL runner-up Dave Kingman, made people sit up and take notice. He also knocked in 123 runs, one more than teammate Rice. Two thirds of a triple crown is better than most.

The hard-hitting Sox, who led the league with a .283 mark, made Tony's job a little easier. He often came up with men on base. And he had a 19-game hitting streak, followed, after one hitless game, by a nine-game streak.

For Tony to remain among the outfield elite, he'll have to cut down on his strikeouts (156) and be more selective at the plate (he walked only 32 times).

11

Outfield
HAROLD
BAINES
CHICAGO WHITE SOX

Before the '84 season, the White Sox were considered a shoo-in for the AL West title. It didn't happen. The Sox flopped to 74–88, but they found a star. Right-fielder Harold Baines clearly proved that he's in the class of the AL's top outfielders.

Chicago fans have been waiting for this. Harold was the first choice in baseball's amateur draft in 1977, then moved quickly through Chicago's farm system, where he's been managed by Chisox skipper Tony LaRussa since '78. It took five full seasons in the major leagues to prove the wisdom of that 1977 draft pick. But now there's no doubt.

Sure, there had been hints before. Baines knocked in 105 runs with 25 homers in 1982. But he never hit for average — until last season. When he finally put it together, he cracked 29 homers and banged in 94 runs for the league's worst hitting team. But he also hit .304, 24 points better than in 1983.

The first six weeks of the 1984 season were an absolute disaster for Baines — and for the Sox. As they fumbled, Harold stumbled. He was hitting less than .200 in late May. Then he got red hot, hitting .373 through mid-August.

The best news? Manager LaRussa thinks Harold can get even better. We agree.

Catcher
LANCE PARRISH
DETROIT TIGERS

Almost any other catcher, off a .237 season at the plate, would fall out of the All-Pro ranking. But not Lance Parrish. The man does everything you'd want a catcher to do — and more.

Though his batting average was 25 points below his .262 lifetime mark, he was the rock-solid leader of the 1984 world champs. He hit with plenty of power (33 homers), his second 30-plus homer year in the last three seasons. He managed his pitching staff effectively and tossed out 33 of 77 runners trying to steal. He also picked three runners off first base, which can really be a rally-killer.

The Tigers look to their 6–3, 220-pound backstop whenever the going gets tough. He usually comes through. Of his 33 homers, at least 10 came in the seventh inning or later. When the Tigers rallied to win late, Lance usually had a piece of the action. He was involved in eight come-from-behind wins. He even stole home against Boston last July, on the delayed end of a double steal.

Parrish fans were disappointed to learn that Lance's 33 homers in '84 didn't break his AL record of 32 homers by a catcher. Some of his '84 round-trippers were hit as a DH. Just one more target to shoot for.

Pitcher
JACK MORRIS
DETROIT TIGERS

Picking this spot is easy. The Tigers' Jack Morris is the American League's Mr. Consistency. When Detroit got off to its super 35–5 start a year ago, Morris was the key, winning 10 of his first 11 decisions.

But that came as no surprise. Year in and year out, the soon-to-be-30-year-old right-hander is the key man on the Detroit staff. He has led the team in victories in each of the last six seasons, a feat that has never been matched by any other Tiger. In that period, Morris won 103 games, the best in the majors by a righty and second only to Philadelphia lefty Steve Carlton, who won 106 games.

When Morris no-hit the White Sox last April 7, he tied the big-league mark for the earliest no-hitter in a season. And when he zoomed to his 10–1 start, it looked like anything was possible in '84. But Jack suffered with arm and elbow woes for the next two months and won only three of his next nine. In fact, he was out of action for a couple of weeks in mid-June, before returning to pitch a one-hitter against Milwaukee. It was his 100th AL victory.

We believe that Jack will come back in excellent health in '85. With his consistent record, he should be the AL mound king again.

MIKE BODDICKER
BALTIMORE ORIOLES

When a minor-leaguer gets a brief visit to the majors, they say he had "a cup of coffee." Mike Boddicker had three years of Baltimore coffee before he got a full meal in 1983. And his two big-league seasons clearly show that Boddicker is ready for a banquet.

The Oriole right-hander was a rookie flash in '83, going 16–8 with a 2.77 ERA, leading Baltimore to a World Series crown. In '84 the Birds flopped, but not because of Mike. His 20–11 mark and sparkling 2.79 ERA were both the top figures in the AL.

The former University of Iowa star (he also played third base there) got off to a horrible start in '84, losing his first three decisions. Then he turned it around, winning six in a row from late July to late August, including a nifty one-hitter against Toronto on August 13.

Boddicker is a master of four pitches: fastball, curve, slider, and change. But that's too simple. Teammates call his change-up a "foshball," which combines a forkball and a change.

Mike hopes that the O's return to the top of the AL East in '85. That's because he's at his best in postseason play. In '83 he did not allow an earned run in 18 Championship Series and World Series innings.

Shifting back to the outfield (from third base) should do wonders for the Dodgers' number-one star, Pedro Guerrero.

National League ALL-PRO TEAM

First Base
KEITH HERNANDEZ
NEW YORK METS

New York is probably America's greatest center of the arts. It has the best opera company, a fine symphony orchestra, and the greatest art museums. But one of the finest artists does his thing outdoors — at Shea Stadium.

He's Keith Hernandez, the Mets' first baseman. Keith does it all, and with a style and grace rarely seen on a baseball diamond.

Keith almost single-handedly kept the once-lowly Metsies in the NL East chase to the final days last year. (Of course, they lost to the once-lowly Cubs.) When Darryl Strawberry struggled, Keith sparkled. When George Foster wasn't hitting, Keith was. When Ron Darling bombed on the mound, Keith bombed enemy pitchers.

By season's end, he'd racked up a .311 average, with 15 homers and 94 RBIs — which drove everyone in the St. Louis area crazy. The deal that brought Hernandez to the Mets from the Cards must go down as one of the all-time steals.

New York fans haven't seen glove work like Keith's in 30 years, since Gil Hodges patrolled first base for the Brooklyn Dodgers. And Hernandez, the one-time NL batting champ, almost never has a slump. He's the key to future Met successes.

18

Second Base
RYNE SANDBERG
CHICAGO CUBS

When the Phillies dealt Ryne Sandberg to the Cubs, there wasn't much noise in either Philadelphia or Chicago. Sandberg hadn't done much in Philly. He certainly couldn't beat out Mike Schmidt at third. And the Cubs hadn't won anything in most fans' lifetimes.

There's plenty of noise now — boos in Philadelphia over the loss of an All-Pro; cheers in Chicago, where Ryne will probably make the Cubbies contenders for years.

Sandberg, a Gold Glove winner in his first season at second base (an all-time NL first), found his bat in '84. Always a good contact hitter, he also found new power last season, finishing with a .314 bat mark, 36 doubles, 19 triples, 19 homers, 84 RBIs, and a league-leading 114 runs scored. Throw in 32 stolen bases, another super year in the field (only six errors and a 62-game streak without a miscue), and the Cubs' first title of any kind in 39 years. Wow! Chicago's Mayor Washington could have new competition for his job.

Cub boss Jim Frey loves Sandberg. "He does everything you could ask of a player," says Frey. "He's an absolute natural — as a hitter, fielder, base runner, and power man. And he has the most accurate throwing arm I've ever seen."

Third Base
MIKE SCHMIDT
PHILADELPHIA PHILLIES

Class always tells. There are some fine young third basemen in the National League. Some of them are quicker than Mike Schmidt. Some are healthier. Some even have "gloves" approaching the old master. But until we're proven wrong, we'll say that Mike Schmidt is No. 1 at third.

Mike has lost a half step or so, and those nagging injuries seem to come more often and last a little longer. There are flecks of gray in the hair. But at the plate, the 35-year-old Schmitty is as fearsome as anyone in the NL.

Mike's book on hitting is one of the minor classics, and he should make a great manager some day — if he can afford the pay cut. Despite those nagging injuries and some beat-up knees (thanks mostly to football), Schmidt got into 151 games a year ago and again led the NL in homers — sharing the title with Atlanta's Dale Murphy (36 round-trippers). For the good-hit, no-pitch Phils, Mike also hit .277 and banged in 106 runs (again sharing league honors, this time with Montreal's Gary Carter). Need more proof? Mike was second in the league in slugging percentage (.536) and fourth in on-base percentage (.383).

As the Phillies try to rebuild, they know that third base is still in old, good hands.

Shortstop
OZZIE
SMITH
ST. LOUIS CARDINALS

Unlike the American League, the National League isn't blessed with a bevy of superstar shortstops. Fortunately, the senior circuit is blessed with Ozzie Smith, considered a national treasure in St. Louis.

Though the AL's No. 1 shortstop, Cal Ripken, Jr., looks more like a big guard in basketball at 6–4½, Ozzie is built like the average guy. At 5–10 and 150 pounds, Ozzie is a large prize in a small package. He hit .257 in '84, 22 points higher than his career average and only one point below his previous big-league high of .258 (with San Diego back in his rookie year, 1978).

But the Cards don't pay Osborne Earl Smith to hit. They pay him to make spectacular fielding plays, which he does routinely. NL Gold Glove voters usually pencil Ozzie into the shortstop spot, then begin worrying about the rest of the roster. He started winning the coveted award after the 1980 season and continues at the top of the league's form charts.

At age 30, Ozzie seems to be at the top of his game. In addition to his superb fielding and improved hitting, Smith added 35 stolen bases to his 206 previous major-league thefts. And, the Wizard of Oz is a Cardinal leader on and off the field. The All-Pro shortstop job is his until he loses it.

21

Outfield
TONY GWYNN
SAN DIEGO PADRES

Patience is a big word in San Diego. The patient fans were finally rewarded last season, after waiting since 1969 for some Padre heroics. And the Padres were rewarded for their wise pick of Tony Gwynn in the third round of the 1981 draft.

A quick trip through the farm system brought Gwynn to the big-league club in less than two years. A .289 mark in 54 games provided hope. But a broken wrist cost him half of the 1983 season. Still, a .309 average in 86 games spurred real hope.

Now he has done it. "I worked hard on my stroke all winter," said Gwynn before the '84 campaign. Maybe the others could learn a lesson from that. Tony led the NL batting race from nearly day one. By early July he was swatting the ball at a mighty .357 clip. Some experts doubted he could keep it up. But he did. His .351 average, in 158 games, was 30 points better than runner-up Lee Lacy of the Pirates.

Gwynn's outfield mates, Kevin McReynolds and Carmelo Martinez, were both rookies. Tony provided great leadership and glove work along with his red-hot bat.

Though Tony hit only five homers, the 5–11, 185-pounder is one of the top natural contact hitters we've seen in a while. He'll do it again in '85.

DALE MURPHY
ATLANTA BRAVES

When Dale Murphy, winner of the NL MVP Award in 1982 and 1983, was struggling at midyear last season, "knowing" heads nodded. "Murphy isn't for real," they said. "He couldn't possibly maintain his pace."

"They," of course, were wrong. The 29-year-old seemed to be motivated by injuries to teammates such as Bob Horner and Glenn Hubbard. Sensing that he had to do more, he raised his average from around .250 to .290, bombed 36 homers (to share the league title with Philadelphia's Mike Schmidt), and knocked in 100 runs. True, he finished "only" ninth in the '84 MVP balloting, but he was the NL's Player of the Month for September.

Everyone knows about Dale's powerful bat. But insiders also know that he's one of the best defensive center fielders in the game, combining excellent speed, sure hands, and a shotgun arm. Speed? Sure. He has 72 stolen bases over the past three seasons. And he has appeared in 495 straight games, the longest current streak in the majors.

The quiet, confident Murph leads more by example than by personal power. Yet he is admired and respected by teammate and opponent alike. Another MVP trophy in '85? Why not?

Outfield
JOSE
CRUZ
HOUSTON ASTROS

At an age (37) when most outfielders are looking for a rocking chair, the Astros' Jose Cruz is just about hitting his stride.

Speaking of stride, of course, Jose has baseball's most unique stride at the plate. As the pitch is on its way, the lefthanded Cruz raises his right (front) leg a foot or so in the air. Few players in baseball history have been successful with this hitting style. Hall of Famer Mel Ott and Japan's home-run king Sadaharu Oh are two examples. Add Cruz to that list.

The Puerto Rico native hit .312 a year ago, raising his average from .238 to .312 over a one-month period, beginning in late June. It was his fifth .300-plus season in 11 years (with another .299 campaign thrown in). It took a month in which he hit better than .500 to do it. But the 6–0, 185-pounder knows what to do.

By season's end, Cruz had led the Astros in games (160 — not bad for an "old" man), at-bats (600), runs (96), hits (187), doubles (28), triples (13), homers (12), RBIs (95), walks (73), and steals (22). Except for game-winning RBIs (Terry Puhl edged Jose, 10–8), it was a clean sweep.

Montreal's Tim Raines has his eye on Cruz's All-Pro spot. But Jose isn't ready to give up yet.

Catcher
GARY CARTER
NEW YORK METS

If Gary Carter thinks the fans loved him in Montreal, he hasn't seen anything yet. If the former Expo can help deliver a title to New York, the newest Met may own the Big Apple. And Carter is looking forward to the opportunity.

Gary is looking forward to 1985, after an outstanding personal performance in '84, which also saw the Expos finish a sorry fifth.

For the fourth time in his 10-year Montreal career, Carter was the team's MVP. No wonder. His numbers were generally the best of his career. With 106 RBIs, he tied the Phils' Mike Schmidt for the league lead. He hit .294, banged out 175 hits, and even had 16 game-winning RBIs. Each of these figures was a career high.

One could argue that the Giants' Bob Brenly came close to matching Carter's figures a year ago. But Brenly is not Carter's equal behind the plate nor has he proven that he can hit with authority regularly.

So Carter goes to New York, hoping for a second shot at a title (his Expos lost to the Dodgers in the 1981 League Championship Series).

One minor Carter question mark: knee surgery a week before the end of the '84 season. But New York can't wait for him.

25

Pitcher
RICK SUTCLIFFE
CHICAGO CUBS

Rick Sutcliffe is unfair to baseball pennant-pickers. Those who tabbed the Cubs near the bottom of the NL East never dreamed that Sutcliffe would show up from Cleveland last June 13 and lead the Cubbies to the top with a 16–1 blow-out. Then just when it looked as if he'd spend '85 in San Diego or Atlanta, he threw us a curve and re-signed with Chicago.

Sutcliffe, who was mediocre (4–5) with the mediocre Indians, returned to the National League, bent on revenge.

Manager Jim Frey admires Rick's competitive nature. "He's tough," says Frey. "Sure, he has the tools — a fine fastball and the other necessary pitches. But a lot of pitchers have the tools and don't do what Rick does. He has that something extra that makes him a winner."

Though Sutcliffe would just as soon forget his fifth-game play-off loss to San Diego, his half season in a Cub uniform was overpowering. After the All-Star break he went 12–0 with a 2.76 ERA, allowing two earned runs or less in 10 of 16 outings. He ran up 14 straight wins (to share a club record), won 20 games for his two teams (only the fourth big-league pitcher ever to do it), and even hit .250, helping his cause. He'll be super again in '85.

Pitcher
DWIGHT
GOODEN
NEW YORK METS

Attention, Printer: Save this page. The Mets' fireballing rookie set the baseball world buzzing last year by establishing just about every record possible for a teenage pitcher.

It came as no surprise to Met manager Dave Johnson. "I saw him at age 17," says Johnson, "and I knew he was very special. What poise!"

Johnson decided to bring Gooden along slowly last year. (General manager Frank Cashen might have preferred to keep Dwight in the minors a bit longer.) So Dwight's early starts went only five or six innings. Still, he began striking out enemy batters with an incredible fastball and a big breaking curve. A fan club in NY began posting K's on the grandstand fence at Shea Stadium every time Gooden registered a strikeout. Dwight kept them busy.

By season's end, the 19-year-old had fanned 276 batters in only 218 innings. His average of 11.39 strikeouts per nine innings was the best in baseball history. He struck out a league-high 16 batters twice in a row, equaling a big-league mark with 32 Ks in two games.

"You don't find many like Dwight," says teammate Keith Hernandez. "I love playing behind him."

Can Angel pitcher Mike "Perfecto" Witt become the first man to hurl back-to-back no-hitters six months apart?

American League TEAM PREVIEWS

AL East
DETROIT TIGERS
1984 Finish: First
1985 Prediction: First

Alan Trammell   Kirk Gibson

There's little chance that the '85 Tigers
will win 35 of their first 40 games and spend
the rest of the year laughing at the other AL
East clubs. There's a very good chance,
however, that Detroit could take it all again
this year.

Manager Sparky Anderson didn't have to
do a lot of managing last time around.
However, this season may prove more
challenging.

Not that there are many problems. Free-
agent relief star Willie Hernandez, the AL's
Cy Young Award winner and MVP, was
looking to open his own bank, which might
not be located in Detroit. The Tigers have
no one to call "our every-day third baseman."

Meanwhile 2B Lou Whitaker (.289) and SS

Alan Trammell (.314) make up the league's best DP combination. 1B Darrell Evans (.232) gets the job done. Catcher Lance Parrish (.237, but 33 homers and 98 RBIs) is one of the best in the business, with a little nod in the direction of Montreal's Gary Carter.

Kirk Gibson (.282, 27 homers) found the joy of World Series stardom to his liking. He should be even better in '85. CF Chet Lemon and LF Larry Herndon are top-notch.

On the mound, Jack Morris (19–11) is one the big leagues' most consistent pitchers. And who can fault Dan Petry (18–8) and Milt Wilcox (17–8)? Ex-Met P Walt Terrell should be a fine addition.

Without Hernandez, the bullpen could be a problem, but vet Aurelio Lopez (10–1) can carry the load. Right-hander Randy O'Neil was impressive in September and could become the needed starter.

It may not be a laugher this time around, but Tiger fans can't wait for the season to get started.

STAT LEADERS — 1984

BATTING
Average: Trammell, .314
Runs: Gibson, 92
Hits: Trammell, 174
Doubles: Trammell, Lemon, 34
Triples: Gibson, 10
Home Runs: Parrish, 33
RBIs: Parrish, 98
Game-Winning RBIs: Gibson, 17
Stolen Bases: Gibson, 29

PITCHING
Wins: Morris, 19
Losses: Morris, 11
Complete Games: Morris, 9
Shutouts: Petry, 2
Saves: Hernandez, 32
Walks: Morris, 87
Strikeouts: Morris, 148

AL East
NEW YORK YANKEES
1984 Finish: Third
1985 Prediction: Second

Butch Wynegar

Joe Cowley

As usual, owner George Steinbrenner played mind games with all of his employees during the off-season, starting with manager Yogi Berra. There was talk about signing every big-name free agent. And there was talk about a 1985 pennant for the Yankees.

The latter probably won't happen. The eight-million-dollar-man, Rickey Henderson, should go very well with offensive powers Dave Winfield and Don Mattingly. But the pitching staff is shaky, at best.

1B Mattingly was the AL's 1984 bat champ. His .343 average edged superathlete Winfield's .340 on the final day of the season.

2B Willie Randolph gives the Yanks a solid leadoff hitter, though there were trade rumors involving his name all fall. Rex Hudler (.292 in AAA) could push Willie — maybe out of the Bronx.

Henderson should solve last year's center-field problem, though the Yanks are still concerned about shortstop. Andre Robertson (.214) never bounced back from his terrible auto accident, but Bobby Meacham showed great promise. Henderson's arrival shakes up the outfield where veterans Ken Griffey (.273) and Omar Moreno (.259), and rookie Vic Mata (.329 in 30 games) will battle for playing time. Griffey could be the lefty DH.

Among the pitchers, Dave Righetti (5–6, 31 saves) starred in the bullpen a year ago. But if he could be replaced in the pen, it'd be a plus for the Yanks, whose pitchers are either old vets: Ron Guidry (10–11), Phil Niekro (16-8), and John Montefusco (5–3); or youngsters: Dennis Rasmussen (9–6) and surprising Joe Cowley (9–2).

STAT LEADERS — 1984

BATTING
Average: Mattingly, .343*
Runs: Winfield, 106
Hits: Mattingly, 207*
Doubles: Mattingly, 44*
Triples: Moreno, 6
Home Runs: Baylor, 27
RBIs: Mattingly, 110
Game-Winning RBIs: Winfield, 13
Stolen Bases: Moreno, 20

*Led league.

PITCHING
Wins: Niekro, 16
Losses: Guidry, 11
Complete Games: Guidry, Niekro, 5
Shutouts: Cowley, Guidry, Niekro, 1
Saves: Righetti, 31
Walks: Niekro, 76
Strikeouts: Niekro, 136

AL East
TORONTO BLUE JAYS
1984 Finish: Second
1985 Prediction: Third

Lloyd Moseby   Willie Upshaw

It doesn't take an elephant's memory to recall the time when a game against Toronto was an automatic win. After years in or near the AL East basement, the Blue Jays put together their best season ever in '84, though their 89–73 mark was a distant second to the champion Tigers.

Manager Bobby Cox, working with a new one-year contract, fields a team blessed with both power and speed, with a good mix of older and younger players.

There's a good dose of talent in the infield where SS Tony Fernandez (.270) made SS Alfredo Griffin expendable. Griffin and OF Dave Collins went to Oakland for super-reliever Bill Caudill.

Youngsters such as 1B Willie Upshaw (.278, 19 homers, 84 RBIs, despite a September slump), CF Lloyd Moseby (.280, 92 RBIs), and LF-RF George Bell (.292, 26 homers, 88 RBIs, and the Jays' team MVP) make the future look brilliant. And OF Jesse Barfield (.284) is sought on the trade mart.

Starting pitching is in decent shape, led by one of the league's best, Dave Stieb (16–8, 2.83 ERA, 198 strikeouts). Righty Doyle Alexander continues to work well in Canada, off his 17–6, 3.13 season. (George Steinbrenner still doesn't want to talk about Alexander!) Caudill (36 saves) makes a rocky bullpen rock-solid, but the Jays still need more hitting out of the third-base and catching spots, and a lefthanded power hitter would help.

There may be help on the way, including OF Mitch Webster, 3B Kelly Gruber, and possibly reliever Stan Clarke.

STAT LEADERS — 1984

BATTING
Average: Bell, .292*
Runs: Moseby, 97
Hits: Garcia, 180
Doubles: Bell, 39
Triples: Collins, Moseby, 15**
Home Runs: Bell, 26
RBIs: Bell, 88
Game-Winning RBIs: Bell, Collins, 11
Stolen Bases: Collins, 60

PITCHING
Wins: Alexander, 17
Losses: Clancy, 15
Complete Games: Alexander, Stieb, 11
Shutouts: Alexander, Leal, Stieb, 2
Saves: Jackson, Key, 10
Walks: Clancy, Stieb, 88
Strikeouts: Stieb, 198

*Collins (.308), Johnson (.304), and Mulliniks (.324) did not qualify.
**Led league.

AL East
BOSTON RED SOX
1984 Finish: Fourth
1985 Prediction: Fourth

Wade Boggs   **Dwight Evans**

New manager John McNamara hopes that
the real Red Sox check in at the start of the
season. Seems the '84 team didn't realize
that the games were for real until late in
May when the Tigers were already un-
catchable.

The ex-California Angels' skipper inher-
its a top-flight starting lineup, with the
most productive outfield in the last 50 years.
Tony Armas (.268, 43 homers, 123 RBIs);
Dwight Evans (.295, 104 RBIs), coming off
knee surgery; and Jim Rice (.280, 122 RBIs)
are the best in the business.

In fact, the team's .283 average was the
best in baseball, by a mile. 2B Marty Bar-
rett took over from the injured Jerry Remy
early in '84, and hit .303. 3B Wade Boggs
swung a .325 stick. In fact, the whole start-

ing lineup is, on paper, as good as anyone's.

Pitching isn't as bad as it might seem. There are some fine young arms, notably Roger Clemens (9–4, before a late-season muscle tear), Bob Nipper (11–6, but 9–2 after July 1), and Oil Can Boyd (12–12, but 10–5 after mid-June). Boyd, Clemens, Bob Ojeda, and Bruce Hurst each struck out 100 or more enemy batters.

What does McNamara need to uplift the Sox? More consistent starters, a big improvement in the bullpen, and depth all around. Look for 3B-OF Steve Lyons to get a real shot this spring, along with speedy Gus Burgess, a good lefty swinger. Righty Jim Dorsey should help the bullpen; and righty Milt Johnson, up from AA, should get a long look.

A major Boston headache: Jim Rice's free-agent status after the '85 season. But McNamara should help this club move up.

STAT LEADERS — 1984

BATTING
Average: Boggs, .325
Runs: Evans, 121*
Hits: Boggs, 203
Doubles: Evans, 37
Triples: Evans, 8
Home Runs: Armas, 43*
RBIs: Armas, 123*
Game-Winning RBIs: Rice, 17
Stolen Bases: Gutierrez, 12

PITCHING
Wins: Boyd, Hurst, Ojeda, 12
Losses: Boyd, Hurst, Ojeda, 12
Complete Games: Boyd, 10
Shutouts: Ojeda, 5**
Saves: Stanley, 22
Walks: Ojeda, 96
Strikeouts: Ojeda, 137

* Led league.   **Tied for league lead.

AL East
BALTIMORE ORIOLES
1984 Finish: Fifth
1985 Prediction: Fifth

Eddie Murray   **Cal Ripken**

The Orioles, like every club in the AL
East, were demoralized by the Tigers' 35–5
start in '84. The O's made a run to finish
second or third, then fell back.

Manager Joe Altobelli has the tools to return toward the top this season — and his
future at the Oriole helm depends on it. The
key will be more offense, where hard-hitting ex-Pirate OF Lee Lacy and ex-Angel OF
Fred Lynn will help a lot.

Starting pitching is in excellent shape.
All-Pro Mike Boddicker (20–11, 2.79 ERA)
leads a staff that includes consistent righties Storm Davis (14–9, 3.14) and one-time
superstar Mike Flanagan (13–13, 3.53). Once
past this trio, Altobelli has to scramble a
little; but the bullpen is improved with the
signing of ex-Angel P Don Aase.

Offensively, Eddie Murray and Cal Ripken will get help from Lacy and Lynn. 1B Murray, who's always in the hunt for All-Pro honors, hit .306 with 29 homers and 110 RBIs in '84. SS Ripken, a fixture as the All-Pro shortstop after only three years in the big leagues, pounded the ball at a .304 clip with 27 homers and 86 RBIs.

Otherwise, there wasn't much. The O's cleaned house during the off-season, dropping vets Ken Singleton, Al Bumbry, Benny Ayala, and Tom Underwood. OF Mike Young (a switch-hitting .252) gave hope for the future, but folks such as Rick Dempsey (.230), Gary Roenicke (.224), John Lowenstein (.237), and others flopped.

Look for young pitchers such as Nate Snell, Ken Dixon, and Mark Brown to get a good look this spring, along with OF Larry Sheets, 2B Vic Rodriguez, and DH Jim Traber. A healthy Tippy Martinez would help the bullpen.

STAT LEADERS — 1984

BATTING
Average: Murray, .306
Runs: Ripken, 103
Hits: Ripken, 195
Doubles: Ripken, 37
Triples: Ripken, 7
Home Runs: Murray, 29
RBIs: Murray, 110
Game-Winning RBIs: Murray, 19*
Stolen Bases: Shelby, 12

PITCHING
Wins: Boddicker, 20*
Losses: Flanagan, 13
Complete Games: Boddicker, 16
Shutouts: Boddicker, 4
Saves: T. Martinez, 17
Walks: Boddicker, Flanagan, 81
Strikeouts: Boddicker, 128

*Led league.

AL East
MILWAUKEE BREWERS
1984 Finish: Seventh
1985 Prediction: Sixth

Jim Gantner   Cecil Cooper

In his previous stay as Milwaukee manager, George Bamberger seemed to work magic on the Brewers. Now, in his second tour, the twice-retired Bambi will have to look high up his sleeve to find the right magic for the current bunch.

Only two years after a near-miss in the World Series, Milwaukee fell to the depths. The club was too old, their starting pitchers (Bamberger's specialty) fell apart, and their power was completely shut off. Check the numbers: only 641 runs, 96 homers, 13 complete games. All were league lows.

Enter Bamberger, with lots of questions. SS Robin Yount (.298, 80 RBIs) could recover from a banged-up shoulder, though he might be forced to leave shortstop for the outfield. 1B Cecil Cooper (.275, 67 RBIs)

must return to top form. 2B Jim Gantner
(.282), one of the AL's best, is back — with
a new four-year contract. C Jim Sundberg
(.261 in 110 games) announced that he
wanted out, which would hurt. Like Cooper,
DH Ted Simmons suffered terribly in '84,
with a pitiful .221 average.

Several late-season additions and
comebacks could key a 1985 bounce-back.
OF Doug Loman, a .276 hitter with 12 RBIs
in 23 games, could help. The club would be
improved if Rollie Fingers, an off-season
free agent, comes back — healthy. Former
Oakland starter Ray Burris (13–10), ob-
tained for top Brewer winner Don Sutton,
must come through.

Former Card and Red OF Paul House-
holder might help provide some of the
needed power, and rookie P Ray Searage
(2–1, 0.70) might be the new bullpen stop-
per Bambi needs.

This club is loaded with question marks,
"what ifs," and "let's hopes."

STAT LEADERS — 1984

BATTING
Average: Yount, .298
Runs: Yount, 105
Hits: Yount, 186
Doubles: Cooper, 28
Triples: Yount, 7
Home Runs: Yount, 16
RBIs: Yount, 80
Game-Winning RBIs: Yount, 9
Stolen Bases: Yount, 14

PITCHING
Wins: Sutton, 14
Losses: Cocanower, 16
Complete Games: Caldwell,
  Haas, 4
Shutouts: Caldwell, Gibson, 1
Saves: Fingers, 23
Walks: Cocanower, 78
Strikeouts: Sutton, 143

AL East
CLEVELAND INDIANS
1984 Finish: Sixth
1985 Prediction: Seventh

Ernie Camacho

Brett Butler

Manager Pat Corrales, who had plenty of talent when managing in Philadelphia, is trying to get by with a lot less in Cleveland. And it hurts.

Actually, were it not for a horrendous pitching staff, the Indians could make up some ground on the AL East leadership. But those pitching arms just don't seem to be around.

Chris Bando (.315) is a better-than-average catcher, with decent backup from Jerry Willard (.224). SS Julio Franco (.286 and a good glove) is first-rate. Brook Jacoby (.264) enjoyed a sparkling rookie year at third, with help from Pat Tabler (.290). There's a logjam at first, which should clear by the end of spring training. Contenders include Mike Hargrove (.267), Tabler, outfielder Joe

Carter (.275), and possibly, Andre Thornton (.271 and 33 home runs), who has signed a new four-year contract with Cleveland.

The only major hole in the infield is second base. But the Tribe has high hopes for U.S. Olympic Team star Cory Snyder, who tore up the Instructional League this past fall.

The outfield is reasonably deep, too, with Mel Hall (.257), Carter, Brett Butler (.269), George Vukovich (.304), and Carmelo Castillo (.261).

Now to the pitching. Outside of staff ace Bert Blyleven (19–7, 2.87, 170 strikeouts), the starters aren't much. The bullpen seems in reasonable shape with surprising Ernie Camacho (5–9, 23 saves) and '84 rookie star Tom Waddell (7–4, with a 24-inning scoreless streak in his last 17 appearances of 1984).

If Rich Behenna (0–3 before surgery) and Neal Heaton (12–15, 5.21) bounce back, there may be hope. But not much.

STAT LEADERS — 1984

BATTING
Average: Vukovich, .304
Runs: Butler, 108
Hits: Franco, 188
Doubles: Thornton, 26
Triples: Butler, 9
Home Runs: Thornton, 33
RBIs: Thornton, 99
Game-Winning RBIs: Thornton, 11
Stolen Bases: Butler, 52

PITCHING
Wins: Blyleven, 19
Losses: Heaton, 15
Complete Games: Blyleven, 12
Shutouts: Blyleven, 4
Saves: Camacho, 23
Walks, Heaton, 75
Strikeouts: Blyleven, 170

AL West
KANSAS CITY ROYALS
1984 Finish: First
1985 Prediction: First

Frank White   **Dan Quisenberry**

Manager Dick Howser starts work on a
new two-year contract, which he richly de-
serves. Thanks to a late-season 44–27 rush,
the Royals won a Western Division championship no one figured on last year.

There's no telling how good this club can
be with Willie Wilson around all year, a
healthy George Brett, continued good work
by the young starting pitchers, and another super season by Dan Quisenberry.

The Royals have built a solid foundation.
1B Steve Balboni bloomed in '84 with 28
homers in 126 games, while doing nicely in
the field. 2B Frank White (.271, despite
nagging injuries) quietly goes about his job,
doing as well as anyone in the league. SS
Onix Concepcion, also bothered by injuries that kept him out of 54 games, is set

after a .282 season at the plate. What can you say about 3B Brett (.284, with knee and hamstring injuries)?

OF Wilson (.301) helped rally the Royals when he returned from his early-season suspension. But the real OF surprises were Darryl Motley (.284) and Pat Sheridan (.283), who won everyday jobs. And Don Slaught (.264) is rock-solid behind the plate.

Pitching was another pleasant surprise. Rookies Mark Gubicza (10–14) and Bret Saberhagen (10–11), a second-year pro, added to the staff that included consistent Bud Black (17–12, 3.12) and ex-Red Charlie Leibrandt (11–7, after going 7–1 in AAA). Larry Gura (12–9) is still sound. And with Quisenberry (6–3, 44 saves, and a Cy Young winner in any league without Willie Hernandez), Royal starters know they can go all out right from the first inning.

A little more power in the clean-up spot will help this club win again.

STAT LEADERS — 1984

BATTING
Average: Wilson, .301
Runs: Wilson, 81
Hits: Wilson, 163
Doubles: Slaught, 27
Triples: Wilson, 9
Home Runs: Balboni, 28
RBIs: Balboni, 77
Game-Winning RBIs: Sheridan, 13
Stolen Bases: Wilson, 47

PITCHING
Wins: Black, 17
Losses: Gubicza, 14
Complete Games: Black, 8
Shutouts: Gubicza, 2
Saves: Quisenberry, 44*
Walks: Gubicza, 75
Strikeouts: Black, 140

*Led league.

AL West
MINNESOTA TWINS
1984 Finish: Second (tied)
1985 Prediction: Second

Frank Viola   **Kent Hrbek**

The Twins were on the verge of great-
ness last summer when a six-game losing
streak flipped them back into a tie for second with California. Now manager Billy
Gardner, who won more than one Manager
of the Year title, has to keep the Twins there.

Minnesota is reasonably sound at most
positions. Hometown boy Kent Hrbek (.311,
27 homers, 107 RBIs) might be the All-Star
first sacker in any league that did not include Eddie Murray and Don Mattingly. 2B
Tim Teufel (.262) does a fine job, but needs
backup help when he's tired. Shortstop is
a problem, though rookie Alvaro Espinosa
might have a shot.

The outfield is led by last year's rookie
flash Kirby Puckett (.296) and ex-Dodger
Mickey Hatcher (.302, 69 RBIs). Catcher Tim

Laudner hit less than .200 most of the season, before landing at .206 as the curtain fell. Barring a trade, look for good-catch, no-hit Jeff Reed to share the chores.

A pair of former Texas Rangers, Mike Smithson and John Butcher, join Frank Viola to give Minnesota a solid starting trio. Viola (18–12) should have won 20, and eventually will. Smithson went 15–13, and Butcher was 13–11 with a 3.44 ERA. Ex-Padre Floyd Chiffer could help.

The bullpen is spelled Ron Davis, who could also be prime trade bait for the Twins. But Davis was 7–11 with 29 saves, and Minnesota should think hard before giving him up.

Left-hander Bryan Oelkers (16–11 in AA ball last year) could join the starting staff. But he's not the whole answer. Lefthanded hitting, another solid reliever, and better play at shortstop and catcher are needed.

STAT LEADERS — 1984

BATTING
Average: Hrbek, .311
Runs: Hrbek, 80
Hits: Hrbek, Hatcher, 174
Doubles: Hatcher, 35
Triples: Hatcher, Puckett,
  Washington, 5
Home Runs: Brunansky, 32
RBIs: Hrbek, 107
Game-Winning RBIs: Brunansky,
  Hrbek, 11
Stolen Bases: Puckett, 14

PITCHING
Wins: Viola, 18
Losses: Smithson, 13
Complete Games:
  Smithson, Viola, 10
Shutouts: Viola, 4
Saves: Davis, 29
Walks: Viola, 73
Strikeouts: Viola, 149

AL West
CHICAGO WHITE SOX
1984 Finish: Fifth (tied)
1985 Prediction: Third

Tom Seaver

Ron Kittle

The Chisox were baseball's surprise team of '84. The surprise was that they didn't win a second straight AL West title. Didn't win it? Heck, from fifth place, they could barely see the leaders. Manager Tony LaRussa, who seemed in trouble late in '84, is now set for '85, with plenty of work ahead.

The starting pitchers should be a major asset, with some big ifs: If Tom Seaver (15–11, only 12 wins short of 300) continues to pitch well at age 41. . . . If Rich Dotson recovers from a 3–11 last-half season, which ruined his year (14–15). . . . If lefties Britt Burns (4–12) and Floyd Bannister (14–11) are up to their high standards. . . . If ex-Padre Tim Lollar pitches the way LaMarr Hoyt used to. The bullpen — never much — still isn't.

The major problem is the offense, which collapsed with a .247 team BA in '84. There are some solid citizens in the lineup, such as OF Harold Baines (an All-Pro, .304, with 29 homers and 94 RBIs), OF Ron Kittle (.215, but 32 homers), and up-and-coming 1B Greg Walker (.294 and 24 homers), the AL's Player of the Month for September.

Greg Luzinski's free-agent status made off-season business tough. But the Bull hit only 13 homers last year, compared with 32 in '83. C-DH Carlton Fisk must improve on his .231 average, and 2B Julio Cruz (.222) must bounce back from foot surgery.

The nucleus for a return to the top is there, and the Sox should get help from OF Daryl Boston (.312, with 15 homers, 19 triples, and 40 stolen bases in AAA) and catcher Joel Skinner, whose injury history makes him a question mark. Tim Hulett should get a shot at Cruz' 2B job. The Sox have great hopes for rookie SS Ozzie Guillen.

STAT LEADERS — 1984

BATTING
Average: Baines, .304
Runs: Baines, 72
Hits: Baines, 173
Doubles: Walker, 29
Triples: Baines, 10
Home Runs: Kittle, 32
RBIs: Baines, 94
Game-Winning RBIs: Baines, 17
Stolen Bases: R. Law, 29

PITCHING
Wins: Seaver, 15
Losses: Hoyt, 18*
Complete Games: Dotson, 14
Shutouts: Seaver, 4
Saves: Reed, 12
Walks: Dotson, 103
Strikeouts: Bannister, 152

*Led league.

AL West
CALIFORNIA ANGELS
1984 Finish: Second (tied)
1985 Prediction: Fourth

Doug DeCinces   **Mike Witt**

For a team that was in the AL West race until the final week last year, the Angels have plenty of problems. Fortunately, veteran manager Gene Mauch was available when '84 manager John McNamara dropped his Angel halo for a pair of Boston red socks.

Mauch will have to work hard. Some of his young players haven't yet proven themselves, and some of his older players may simply be too old.

Take 39-year-old 1B Rod Carew, for example. The frequent AL bat champ slumped to .295 (not bad for mere mortals), going under .300 for the first time since 1969. 2B Bobby Grich was mired at .217 until a batting adjustment helped him raise his average to .256. 3B Doug DeCinces doesn't show his 34 years (he hit .269 with 82 RBIs), but SS Dick Schofield is a minus at the plate, with his .193 average.

The off-season loss of free-agent CF Fred Lynn (.271, 23 homers) doesn't help matters. But the outfield is in decent shape with team MVPs Juan Beniquez (.336) and Brian Downing (.275, 91 RBIs). Reggie Jackson's 25-homer, 81-RBI season marked a fine comeback. But will it last? OF Gary Pettis must hit better than .227, and C Bob Boone's .202 is totally unacceptable if the Angels are to challenge. OF Mike Brown showed flashes of power, and rookie Chris Clark (.332 in AAA) could help.

Pitching is in fair shape, with a youngster like Ron Romanick (12–12) and vets such as Mike "Perfect Game" Witt (15–11, 3.47) and Geoff Zahn (13–10).

If Mauch can find a fourth starter and relief help for Luis Sanchez (9–7, 11 saves), he'll earn his money. It isn't likely.

STAT LEADERS — 1984

BATTING
Average: Downing, .275*
Runs: Lynn, 84
Hits: Downing, 148
Doubles: Downing, Lynn, 28
Triples: Pettis, 6
Home Runs: Jackson, 25
RBIs: Downing, 91
Game-Winning RBIs: DeCinces, 12
Stolen Bases: Pettis, 48

PITCHING
Wins: Witt, 15
Losses: John, 13
Complete Games:
  Romanick, 8
Shutouts: Zahn, 5**
Saves: Sanchez, 11
Walks: Witt, 84
Strikeouts: Witt, 196

*Beniquez (.336) did not qualify.   **Tied for league lead.

AL West
SEATTLE MARINERS
1984 Finish: Fifth (tied)
1985 Prediction: Fifth

Mark Langston   **Alvin Davis**

Off a 15–12 September, the best September in Mariner history, Chuck Cottier gets a full-year shot at managing the still weak M's. If he can hang on for a couple of years and the youngsters continue to improve, Cottier could become a hero in Seattle.

Start with 1B Alvin Davis, last year's Rookie of the Year. Alvin hits with power (.284, 27 homers). When he learns how to hit off-speed pitches, he'll be murder. He drew 16 intentional walks last year, a rookie record. There's also good depth in the middle of the infield, with 2Bs Jack Perconte (.294) and newcomer Harold Reynolds, and SSs Spike Owen (.245) and Danny Tartabull. Look for some trading action.

Pitching is in fairly able hands. AL

strikeout king, rookie lefty Mark Langston (17–10, 3.40), might have attracted more notice were not Dwight Gooden setting records for the Mets. Jim Beattie (12–16, 3.41) is solid if he comes back from shoulder problems, and Matt Young (6–8, but 3–0 with a 1.11 ERA after returning from the minors) should start regularly. There's also 6–8 (that's his height, not his record) Lee Gutterman, the tallest lefty hurler ever.

The outfield must produce more punch for Seattle to win. If Gorman Thomas bounces back from shoulder surgery, they'll get it. But Thomas may be only a DH after the rotator-cuff problem. OF Phil Bradley (.301) was spectacular after the All-Star break and has shown great range in the field.

In addition to Tartabull and Reynolds, look for Darnell Coles and Jim Presley to get some big-league infield time, with Dave Valle and Orlando Mercado trying for a catching spot.

STAT LEADERS — 1984

BATTING
Average: Perconte, .294
Runs: Perconte, 93
Hits: Perconte, 180
Doubles: Cowens, Davis, 34
Triples: Owen, 8
Home Runs: Davis, 27
RBIs: Davis, 116
Game-Winning RBIs: Davis, 13
Stolen Bases: Perconte, 29

PITCHING
Wins: Langston, 17
Losses: Beattie, 16
Complete Games: Beattie, 12
Shutouts: Beattie, Langston, 2
Saves: Stanton, 8
Walks: Langston, 118*
Strikeouts: Langston, 204*

*Led league.

AL West
OAKLAND A'S
1984 Finish: Fourth
1985 Prediction: Sixth

Dave Kingman   Carney Lansford

Everyone in Oakland was delighted when Jackie Moore, who replaced Steve Boros as manager last May, got the green light for a full season in '85. But unless Moore can somehow discover some starting pitchers, his stay may be brief.

Starting pitching is only one of several major Oakland problems, but it is the most obvious. With big winner Ray Burris gone, aging ex-Brewer Don Sutton must do the job. The A's got rid of Lary Sorenson (6–13) and Jeff Jones (0–3), and were thinking about cutting 41-year-old Tom Burgmeier. With starters such as Bill Krueger (10–10, 4.75) and Steve McCatty (8–14, 4.76), is it any wonder that now-departed Bill Caudill had 36 saves?

Things are better on offense. 3B Carney

Lansford (.300) decided to stay with Oakland. OF Dwayne Murphy (.256, 33 homers) joined comeback star DH Dave Kingman (.268, 35 homers) as the first 30-homer teammates in 15 years. 2B Tony Phillips (.266) will replace the apparently retired Joe Morgan (.244). Ex-Blue Jays Dave Collins and Alfredo Griffin should win outfield and shortstop spots respectively. But OF Rickey Henderson (.293, 66 steals) will be greatly missed.

Without Caudill, Keith Atherton (7-6, 4.33) and possibly '84 rookie lefty Dave Leiper (1–0) must perform in the bullpen. And the New York Yankees sent some fine young pitchers, most notably Jay Howell and Jose Rijo.

There are also a couple of talented youngsters on the Oakland farm, such as SS Steve Kiefer and C Mickey Tettleton. But they won't be enough to keep Oakland in the title hunt.

STAT LEADERS — 1984

BATTING

Average: Lansford, .300
Runs: Henderson, 113
Hits: Lansford, 179
Doubles: Phillips, 24
Triples: Heath, Lansford, 5
Home Runs: Kingman, 35
RBIs: Kingman, 118
Game-Winning RBIs: Kingman, 14
Stolen Bases: Henderson, 66*

PITCHING

Wins: Burris, 13
Losses: McCatty, 14
Complete Games: Burris, 5
Shutouts: Burris, Young, 1
Saves: Caudill, 36
Walks: Burris, 90
Strikeouts: Burris, 93

*Led league.

AL West
TEXAS RANGERS
1984 Finish: Seventh
1985 Prediction: Seventh

Charlie Hough

Larry Parrish

For all but three weeks of the 26-week 1984 season, the Rangers occupied the AL West cellar. Just getting out will be tough for manager Doug Rader, three-year contract and all.

The Texans' problems are too numerous to mention, but they include shoddy defense (particularly in the infield), a poverty-stricken bullpen (would you believe only 21 saves?), and so-so catching.

The plusses are solid offense and fine outfielding. Looking at the offensive numbers, it's hard to believe this was a last-place club. Check 3B Buddy Bell (.315, 83 RBIs, his second-best year in a long career). Larry Parrish knocked in 101 runs and swatted 42 doubles, second in the AL. OF Gary Ward banged in 97 runs. 1B Pete

O'Brien had 80 RBIs. Former Blue Jay DH Cliff Johnson may also help.

On the other hand, the middle of the infield was awful. In 338 at-bats, 2B Wayne Tolleson knocked in only nine runs. 2B-SS Curtis Wilkerson committed 30 errors. And promising SS Jeff Kunkel (.204), son of umpire Bill Kunkel, needs another year of minor-league play.

On the mound, knuckle-balling Charlie Hough went 16–14 with a 3.76 ERA. And Frank Tanana's 15–15 and 3.25 ERA were impressive. Both could have been much better had they gotten some bullpen help. Outside of Dave Schmidt (6–6, 12 saves, 2.56), there was absolutely nothing.

Neither Dave Stewart (7–14, 4.73) nor Danny Darwin (8–12, 3.94) figured to be around once Rader cleaned out his bullpen. The Rangers hope that P Al Lachowicz, who suffered with arm trouble in the minors, is healthy and ready to help.

STAT LEADERS — 1984

BATTING

Average: Bell, .315
Runs: Ward, 97
Hits: Parrish, 175
Doubles: Parrish, 42
Triples: Ward, 7
Home Runs: Parrish, 22
RBIs: Parrish, 101
Game-Winning RBIs: Parrish, 11
Stolen Bases: Tolleson, 22

PITCHING

Wins: Hough, 16
Losses: Tanana, 15
Complete Games: Hough, 17*
Shutouts: Darwin, Hough,
   Tanana, 1
Saves: Schmidt, 12
Walks: Hough, 94
Strikeouts: Hough, 164

*Led league.

For the Mets to win the 1985 NL East flag, they'll need another dynamite season from graceful, clutch-hitting Keith Hernandez.

National League
TEAM PREVIEWS

NL East
NEW YORK METS
1984 Finish: Second
1985 Prediction: First

Darryl Strawberry

Jesse Orosco

Met fans were joyous last summer when their darlings (including Ron Darling) sat atop the NL East for a couple of months before falling to the Cubs. Their young players give promise of more thrills to come.

Start with 20-year-old Dwight Gooden, whose swift fastball and giant curve fanned 276 batters in 218 innings. Hailed as the second coming of, well, some immortal, Gooden was 17–9 for the year with seven complete games and three shutouts. Another rookie, Ron Darling (12–9), won seven straight before faltering — which helped speed the Mets' August decline. The final flop was also triggered by a shoulder injury to reliever Doug Sisk (1–3, 15 saves), which added to the pressure on top reliever Jesse Orosco (10–6, 31 saves). If Sisk doesn't come back, look for Wes Gardner (1–1) to become the No. 2 man in the pen. In addition, Sid Fernandez (6–6) must improve.

NL All-Pro C Gary Carter (.294, 27 homers), in from Montreal, gives the Mets solid backstopping and a needed power source on offense.

The outfield is two-thirds complete, with vet George Foster (.269, 86 RBIs) helping third-year man Darryl Strawberry (.251, but 26 homers and 97 RBIs). If Strawberry lives up to his notices, the Mets will be extra tough. CF Mookie Wilson is questionable.

No questions at first, where the majors' best, Keith Hernandez (.311, 94 RBIs) holds forth. The rest of the infield is unsettled, with 1984 3B Hubie Brooks, seen as the '85 SS, off to the Expos. Late-season pickup Ray Knight or ex-Tiger Howard Johnson could be the third sacker, with Kelvin Chapman a slight choice at 2B. Manager Dave Johnson still needs bench strength.

STAT LEADERS — 1984

BATTING
Average: Hernandez, .311
Runs: Wilson, 88
Hits: Hernandez, 171
Doubles: Wilson, 28
Triples: Wilson, 10
Home Runs: Strawberry, 26
RBIs: Strawberry, 97
Game-Winning RBIs: Hernandez, 17
Stolen Bases: Wilson, 46

PITCHING
Wins: Gooden, 17
Losses: Terrell, 12
Complete Games: Gooden, 7
Shutouts: Gooden, 3
Saves: Orosco, 31
Walks: Darling, 104
Strikeouts: Gooden, 276*

*Led league.

NL East
CHICAGO CUBS
1984 Finish: First
1985 Prediction: Second

Leon Durham   Bob Dernier

The Cubs ended a 39-year losing streak by winning the NL East a year ago. The joy was short-lived as the Padres came from two games behind to win the league title in five. Still, the Cubs produced great excitement in the Windy City with their surprise half pennant. A repeat probably won't take 39 more years, but a lack of starting pitching could create a problem for '85.

Dennis Eckersley (10–8) and Steve Trout (13–7) will be back. So will Cy Young Award winner Rick Sutcliffe (16–1 beginning June 14). The Cubs had to open the bank vault to sign the free agent, but he's worth it. Without him the Cubs would have been in trouble that even a fine bullpen (Lee Smith, at 9–7 with 33 saves, and friends) couldn't overcome. Ex-Yank Ray Fontenot will help.

The rest of the crowd is solid, with the exception of shortstop, where Larry Bowa (.223, 17 RBIs) has seen better days. 1B Leon "Bull" Durham (.279) had a career-high 23 homers and 96 RBIs. 2B Ryne Sandberg was a shoo-in MVP off a dream season (.314, up 53 points from '83; 19 triples; and 36 doubles). 3B Ron "Penguin" Cey (.240) showed the Dodgers that they gave up on him too soon (25 homers, 97 RBIs).

Speedy Bob Dernier (.278) stole 45 bases (the most by a Cub since 1907) and led an outstanding outfield (left fielder Gary Matthews and right fielder Keith Moreland). Matthews, a genuine leader, had 19 game-winning hits. C Jody Davis (.256) has really tightened his defense behind the plate.

If pitching problems persist, manager Jim Frey may turn to rookies Ron Meridith and Bill Earley. OF Bill Hatcher might help, too.

STAT LEADERS — 1984

BATTING
Average: Sandberg, .314
Runs: Sandberg, 114*
Hits: Sandberg, 200
Doubles: Sandberg, 36
Triples: Sandberg, 19**
Home Runs: Cey, 25
RBIs: Cey, 97
Game-Winning RBIs:
    Matthews, 19*
Stolen Bases: Dernier, 45

PITCHING
Wins: Sutcliffe, 16
Losses: Ruthven, 10
Complete Games: Sutcliffe, 7
Shutouts: Sutcliffe, 3
Saves: Smith, 33
Walks: Trout, 59
Strikeouts: Sutcliffe, 155

*Led league.   **Tied for league lead.

NL East
PHILADELPHIA PHILLIES
1984 Finish: Fourth
1985 Prediction: Third

Steve Carlton

Juan Samuel

Despite crippling injuries to numerous key players, the 1984 Phillies remained in the title chase until September. No team in baseball has won back-to-back division titles in the past three seasons. So history, which hurt the Phils in '84, may help them catch the Cubs in '85.

New manager John Felske has a solid group to work with. 3B Mike Schmidt is still the NL's best (.277, 36 homers, 106 RBIs) at the hot corner. And lefty Steve Carlton (13–7) still scares opponents.

The Phillies' 1984 superrook, 2B Juan Samuel, nearly became only the sixth player in history with more than 70 steals (72) and 70 RBIs (he wound up with 69). He set rookie records for game-winning RBIs (13), steals — and strikeouts, while committing 33 errors and failing to turn enough double plays. On balance, he's a big plus. 1B Len Matuszek missed 48 games, but hit .248 with some power and became the team's prime pinch hitter.

OF Von Hayes finally bloomed, hitting .292 with 16 homers. OF Garry Maddox (.282) missed most of the last two months. But OF Jeff Stone (.362) sparkled late.

There's young talent. Ozzie Virgil (.261) is set to catch; rookie SS Steve Jeltz will probably join Samuel as the DP combo. P Don Carman, OF John Russell, IF Francisco Melendez, and IF Rich Schu will also get shots.

The mound staff needs a healthy John Denny (7–7), possibly another starter, and new and/or improved bullpen work to go along with Al Holland, who suffered at 5–10 with 29 saves.

This club has a true shot at the top.

STAT LEADERS — 1984

BATTING
Average: Hayes, .292
Runs: Samuel, 105
Hits: Samuel, 191
Doubles: Samuel, 36
Triples: Samuel, 19*
Home Runs: Schmidt, 36*
RBIs: Schmidt, 106*
Game-Winning RBIs: Schmidt, Samuel, 13
Stolen Bases: Samuel, 72

PITCHING
Wins: Koosman, 14
Losses: Koosman, 15
Complete Games: Koosman, Rawley, 3
Shutouts: Koosman, Hudson, 1
Saves: Holland, 29
Walks: Carlton, 79
Strikeouts: Carlton, 163

*Tied for league lead.

NL East
ST. LOUIS CARDINALS
1984 Finish: Third
1985 Prediction: Fourth

Willie McGee · Joaquin Andujar

The Cards finished strong in '84, getting within hailing distance of the Cubs and the Mets. This strong finish bodes well for the future.

Problem is, we're still not sure the Cards will find their bats, which were missing for much of last year. Try this number on for size: OF George Hendrick led the club in RBIs — with only 69! And Hendrick played in only 120 games. But Hendrick has been sent to Pittsburgh for P John Tudor (12–11).

Without Bruce Sutter, the bullpen will be in trouble. Sutter had 45 saves to go with his five wins (and seven losses), with a sparkling 1.54 ERA. Joaquin Andujar was superb, with a 20–14 record (the NL's only 20-game winner). Lefty Dave LaPoint was solid all the way (12–10, 3.96). Neil Allen and

Ricky Horton will hope to replace Sutter in the bullpen.

The Cards felt that Tommy Herr (who made only six errors in 145 games) would solve their second-base spot. But Tommy demanded a trade, and the club was obliged to make one. Lonnie Smith (a disappointing .250 and a liability in the outfield) was also a trade possibility. 3B Terry Pendleton (.324; .358 hitting lefty) was a pleasant surprise and started 65 straight games at the hot corner. To obtain needed help, practically any Cardinal could be dealt, including Lonnie Smith (but never All-Pro SS Ozzie Smith), Hendrick, Allen, and Andy Van Slyke.

Manager Whitey Herzog may look to rookie Vince Coleman (.261 in the minors with 101 steals) for outfield help. Ex-Phillie Mike Lavalliere could help behind the plate.

STAT LEADERS — 1984

BATTING
Average: McGee, .291
Runs: McGee, 82
Hits: McGee, 166
Doubles: Hendrick, 28
Triples: McGee, 11
Home Runs: Green, 15
RBIs: Hendrick, 69
Game-Winning RBIs:
   Hendrick, 16
Stolen Bases: L. Smith, 50

PITCHING
Wins: Andujar, 20*
Losses: Andujar, 14
Complete Games: Andujar, 12
Shutouts: Andujar, 4**
Saves: Sutter, 45*
Walks: LaPoint, 77
Strikeouts: Andujar, 147

*Led league.   **Tied for league lead.

NL East
MONTREAL EXPOS
1984 Finish: Fifth
1985 Prediction: Fifth

Tim Raines   Charlie Lea

Science fiction's Buck Rogers flits about the cosmos, dodging villains and performing good deeds. The real world's Buck Rodgers, the new manager of the Expos, will find it a little harder to fly high in the NL East, especially without All-Pro C Gary Carter (.294, 106 RBIs), now gone to the Mets.

There's decent talent, especially on the mound, in the outfield, and behind the plate. The staff's 3.31 ERA was the NL's third lowest. And you'd be hard-pressed to find an outfielder quicker than Tim Raines.

Raines suffered in center field and will return to left in '85. His arm is the kind opposing base runners love to run on. But Timmy does some decent running himself, with 75 steals and 38 doubles, both league-leading figures, to go along with a sparkling .309 average. RF Terry Francona should be healthy, and former Met Herm Winningham (.407 in 14 games) should help.

1B Dan Driessen hit .254 with nine homers and 32 RBIs in 51 Expo games after coming over from Cincinnati. Despite Dan's free-agent status, the Expos expected to re-sign him. That still leaves tremendous holes at short and second. Ex-White Sox Vance Law and ex-Met Hubie Brooks should fit right in.

Pitching should be a plus, with solid starters in Bill Gullickson (12–9, 3.61) and Charlie Lea (15–10, 2.89). Gullickson was particularly strong the last half of '84. The able bullpen staff is led by Jeff Reardon (7–7, 2.90, 23 saves). The one-time Met righty is now Montreal's career-saves leader. Lefty Jeff Hesketh (12–3 in AAA) should help the staff. But it will take more than this to return Montreal to the top.

STAT LEADERS — 1984

BATTING

Average: Raines, .309
Runs: Raines, 106
Hits: Raines, 192
Doubles: Raines, 38*
Triples: Raines, 9
Home Runs: Carter, 27
RBIs: Carter, 106*
Game-Winning RBIs: Carter, 16
Stolen Bases: Raines, 75**

PITCHING

Wins: Lea, 15
Losses: Rogers, 15
Complete Games: Lea, 8
Shutouts: Smith, 2
Saves: Reardon, 23
Walks: Rogers, 78
Strikeouts: Lea, 123

*Tied for league lead.   **Led league.

NL East
PITTSBURGH PIRATES
1984 Finish: Sixth
1985 Prediction: Sixth

Bill Madlock   Rick Rhoden

The Bucs, a preseason favorite for the 1984
division crown, flopped badly. Manager
Chuck Tanner, whose contract runs for three
more seasons, decided to clean house,
starting with some veteran coaches.
Coaches? Well, you have to start some-
where.

No one could blame Chuck for cleaning
out his toothless bullpen. Even with one-
time superstar Kent Tekulve (3–9, 13 saves),
the whole crew managed only 34 saves.

Fortunately, the Bucs have excellent
starters — and might use some in trades
or even the bullpen. Lefty John Candelaria
(12–11, 2.72) is a major relief candidate, but
Candy wants more money to work more
often. Righty Don Robinson (5–6), 10 saves)
could be the relief king, with solid righty

Rick Rhoden (14–9), lefty Larry McWilliams (12–11, 2.93), and Jose DeLeon (7–13) getting most of the starts. Even without bullpen help, the Bucs' team ERA (3.11) was the majors' best in '84.

Slugging 1B Jason Thompson (.254, 17 homers) could also be dealt, along with his $800,000 salary. If Thompson leaves, 3B Bill Madlock (.253 in an injury-riddled season) could move to first. That would move SS Dale Berra (.222) to third, where he might do a better job. 2B Johnny Ray, who tied a record with six straight game-winning RBIs, is first-rate. Either Rafael Belliard or Ron Wotus could join the Pirate infield.

The young outfield includes ex-Met farmhand Marvel Wynne (.266), defensive ace Joe Orsulak, and Benny Distefano. OF George Hendrick (.277), in from St. Louis for P John Tudor, should help.

Pitchers Mike Bielecki (19–3) and Alfonso Pulido (18–6) could jump from AAA.

STAT LEADERS — 1984

BATTING
Average: Lacy, .321
Runs: Pena, Wynne, 77
Hits: Wynne, 174
Doubles: Ray, 38*
Triples: Wynne, 11
Home Runs: Thompson, 17
RBIs: Pena, 78
Game-Winning RBIs: Thompson, 11
Stolen Bases: Wynne, 24

PITCHING
Wins: Rhoden, 14
Losses: DeLeon, 13
Complete Games:
  McWilliams, 7
Shutouts: Rhoden, 3
Saves: Tekulve, 13
Walks: DeLeon, 92
Strikeouts: DeLeon, 153

*Tied for league lead.

NL West
SAN DIEGO PADRES
1984 Finish: First
1985 Prediction: First

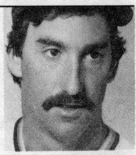

Steve Garvey   Eric Show

You may not recognize the Padres this summer. They'll be wearing new uniforms, featuring pinstripes. And they'll be flying their first NL championship flag.

The NL West title came fairly easy for the '84 Padres, though they really proved themselves when they rallied from 0–2 to top the Cubs in the play-offs. But the Tigers exposed San Diego's modest starting pitchers during the World Series. The result was the dropping of pitching coach Norm Sherry.

The bulk of the Padre pitching staff will return, including Eric Show (15–9) and Mark Thurmond (14–8). Tim Lollar (11–13) is off to Chicago for the Sox' '83 Cy Young winner LaMarr Hoyt. If Hoyt bounces back, watch out! The fourth starter, Ed Whitson (14–8, a personal-best 3.24 ERA), was a winter free agent. As long as Goose Gossage (10–6, 25 saves) is ready to back them up, the Padres will win a lot. And Andy Hawkins (8–9) really grew up in postseason play.

Still, there's a need for another starter. Minor-leaguers such as righty Ed Wojna and lefty Ray Hayward may not be ready.

Heavy-hitting Tony Gwynn (.351, the major-league leader) paces the outfield. Carmelo Martinez (.250) improved considerably at the plate. Kevin McReynolds (.278) was missed badly after he was hurt in the league Championship Series.

The infield is solid, with Steve Garvey (.284) at first, Alan Wiggins (.258) proving himself at second despite some routine errors, Garry Templeton at short, and aging Graig Nettles at third. Despite a .228 average, Nettles smacked 20 homers. Terry Kennedy (.240) is a key behind the plate.

STAT LEADERS — 1984

BATTING
Average: Gwynn, .351*
Runs: Wiggins, 106
Hits: Gwynn, 213*
Doubles: Martinez, 28
Triples: Gwynn, 10
Home Runs: McReynolds, Nettles, 20
RBIs: Garvey, 86
Game-Winning RBIs: Garvey, 15
Stolen Bases: Wiggins, 70

PITCHING
Wins: Show, 15
Losses: Lollar, 13
Complete Games: Show, Lollar, Dravecky, 3
Shutouts: Lollar, Dravecky, 2
Saves: Gossage, 25
Walks: Lollar, 105
Strikeouts: Lollar, 131

*Led league.

NL West
ATLANTA BRAVES
1984 Finish: Second (tied)
1985 Prediction: Second

Rafael Ramirez   **Rick Mahler**

Braves' owner Ted Turner is a tough guy to work for. He fired skipper Joe Torre after the one-time slugger enjoyed more than modest success. And he gave Joe's successor, Eddie Haas, only a one-year deal, after 20 years in the Braves' organization.

With any kind of luck, Haas may earn a longer pact next time around. Having Bruce Sutter, the NL's top reliever, in the fold helps make up for the apparent loss of 3B Bob Horner. And having P Pascual Perez around all season (14–8, after an early-season suspension) can't hurt.

CF Dale Murphy (.290, 36 homers) didn't quite pull off a third straight MVP Award, but he's a potent force around whom Haas can build. If much-heralded Brad Komminsk (.203) can live up to his notices, the

Braves will have a wonderful outfield.

SS Rafael Ramirez (.266) was among the league's hitting leaders until the All-Star break. He'll be pushed by rookie Paul Zuvella, who will also get a shot at Glen Hubbard's (.234) second-base job. 3B Ken Oberkfell, who filled in for Horner, may lose out altogether if Paul Runge can make it. Ex-Yank C Rick Cerone should help.

The Braves need some healthy pitchers to move back to the top. Pete Falcone (5–7) has retired, Terry Forster (2–0 and on the disabled list three times) has a weight problem. Craig McMurtry (9–17) was horrible during the middle of the season. But with all their troubles, some good came of it. Rick Mahler (13–10) had an outstanding second half and Donnie Moore (4–5) came along well. Rick Camp (8–6) is solid. Pitching coach Johnny Sain could be a key man for manager Haas.

STAT LEADERS — 1984

BATTING

Average: Murphy, .290
Runs: Murphy, 94
Hits: Murphy, 176
Doubles: Murphy, 32
Triples: Murphy, 8
Home Runs: Murphy, 36*
RBIs: Murphy, 100
Game-Winning RBIs: Murphy, 13
Stolen Bases: Washington, 21

PITCHING

Wins: Perez, 14
Losses: McMurtry, 17
Complete Games: Mahler, 12
Shutouts: Mahler, Perez, 1
Saves: Moore, 16
Walks: McMurtry, 102
Strikeouts: Perez, 145

*Tied for league lead.

NL West
LOS ANGELES DODGERS
1984 Finish: Fourth
1985 Prediction: Third

Fernando Valenzuela   Pedro Guerrero

Talk about the luck of Lasorda! Armed
with the first multiyear manager's contract
in the last 50 years of Dodger baseball,
manager Tommy saw his Dodgers flop during the second half of '84. But Lasorda is
back on the job, as optimistic as ever.

His optimism may have no basis in fact.
He has some talented players, but too few
of them were healthy a year ago. Fifteen
Dodgers spent time on the disabled list, including three of them twice each. And P
Steve Howe, who was suspended for drug
use in '84, hurt his elbow during the off-
season, and may be questionable.

The fact that the Dodgers were last in the
league in hitting last year doesn't help. The
pitchers, though talented, need help. Ale-
jandro Pena (12–6) was the NL's ERA champ

(2.48). Fernando Valenzuela (12–17) worked more innings than any NL pitcher, except for Joaquin Andujar. Orel Hershiser, given an opportunity to start because of injuries to Jerry Reuss (5–7) and Rick Honeycutt (10–9), sparkled with a 11–8, 2.66 record.

Pedro Guerrero (.303) should be even better, now that his 3B experiment is over. Mike Marshall (.257) continues to mature and shows decent power. 1B Greg Brock (.225), once the apparent successor to Steve Garvey, may never make it, though Sid Bream (.342 in AAA) seems ready. Catching is questionable, with Mike Scioscia (.273) the best of the lot after rotator-cuff surgery. C Jack Fimple (.251 in AAA) had off-season elbow surgery, and Steve Yeager (.228) tries to bounce back from a broken leg. The Dodgers need a solid third sacker, a healthy Steve Howe, good health, a sound Dave Anderson, and a little Tom Lasorda luck.

STAT LEADERS — 1984

BATTING
Average: Guerrero, .303
Runs: Guerrero, 85
Hits: Guerrero, 162
Doubles: Guerrero, 29
Triples: Landreaux, 5
Home Runs: Marshall, 21
RBIs: Guerrero, 72
Game-Winning RBIs: Marshall, 10
Stolen Bases: Sax, 34

PITCHING
Wins: Welch, 13
Losses: Valenzuela, 17
Complete Games:
   Valenzuela, 12
Shutouts: Pena, Hershiser, 4**
Saves: Niedenfuer, 11
Walks: Valenzuela, 106*
Strikeouts: Valenzuela, 240

*Led league.   **Tied for league lead.

NL West
HOUSTON ASTROS
1984 Finish: Second (tied)
1985 Prediction: Fourth

Jerry Mumphrey   **Terry Puhl**

According to manager Bob Lillis, the key to the 1985 Astro season is consistency. He might also have mentioned better starting pitching, a new dose of power, and a healthy Dickie Thon.

The Astros recovered (almost) from a disastrous 1984 start to finish in second place in the NL West. An eye injury to Thon during the fifth game of the season (he never returned) really shook up the club, despite the excellent play of backup SS Craig Reynolds (.260). The bats lay dormant for most of the first two months. But the Astros bounced back during the second half of the season, led by the hitting of 1B Enos Cabell (.310), 2B Bill Doran (.261, 11 triples), and 3B Phil Garner (.278).

The outfield is outstanding, led by ageless (actually 37-year-old) Jose Cruz (.312, and among the league leaders in many categories). RF Terry Puhl (.301) and CF Jerry Mumphrey (.290) complement Cruz well though switch-hitting Mumphrey hit only .247 from the right side. Neither catcher, Mark Bailey (.212) nor Alan Ashby (.262) did a major-league job, and the Astros need help here.

Starting pitching could also use a new face or two. Fireballing Nolan Ryan spent six weeks on the disabled list, though he still compiled 197 strikeouts. Ancient Joe Niekro (16–12), inspired by Yankee brother Phil, hurled nearly 250 innings. And lefty Bob Knepper (15–10) had 11 complete games. Righty Jeff Heathcock, a top prospect a year ago, missed nearly all of 1984 with a leg injury, and could bounce back. The bullpen is deep, though there's no single star. Jeff Calhoun and Mark Ross could challenge Frank DiPino, Bill Dawley, Dave Smith, Julio Solano, and Jose Sambito.

STAT LEADERS — 1984

BATTING
Average: Cruz, .312
Runs: Cruz, 96
Hits: Cruz, 187
Doubles: Cruz, 28
Triples: Cruz, 13
Home Runs: Cruz, 12
RBIs: Cruz, 95
Game-Winning RBIs: Puhl, 10
Stolen Bases: Cruz, 22

PITCHING
Wins: Niekro, 16
Losses: Niekro, 12
Complete Games: Knepper, 11
Shutouts: Knepper, 3
Saves: DiPino, 14
Walks: Niekro, 89
Strikeouts: Ryan, 197

NL West
SAN FRANCISCO GIANTS
1984 Finish: Sixth
1985 Prediction: Fifth

Bob Brenly

Jeff Leonard

Jim Davenport, a one-time Giant third sacker and one of baseball's best hitting teachers, now gets a shot at teaching the whole game. Though offense is Jim's specialty, it isn't his team's problem.

Actually, the Giants bang the ball pretty well, despite their cellar finish. Davenport may preserve Jack Clark's health by moving Clark (.320 in 57 games before a season-ending knee injury) to first base. That still leaves a potent outfield, featuring exciting Chili Davis (.315), solid Jeff Leonard (.302, 86 RBIs), and Dan Gladden (.351 in 86 Giants' games after .397 in 59 AAA games). Wow!

A healthy Manny Trillo (.254 in only 98 games) would help strengthen an infield that was weak defensively. Chris Brown, a

.283 hitter in AAA, will get a full shot at 3B, where he had a brief trial last September. Johnnie LeMaster (.217), Duane Kuiper (.200), and John Rabb (.195) aren't very exciting. And what will Davenport do with Scot Thompson (.306) if he moves Clark to first? Catcher Bob Brenly, starting his fourth season after surgery on both knees, really bloomed a year ago, with 20 homers, 80 RBIs, and a .291 average.

Even if Davenport can shore up his defense, he still has problems with his pitching staff. Only Mike Krukow (11–12) won as many as 10 games and he was awful in August and September. The rest of the starters, including righty Jeff Robinson (7–15), righty Bill Laskey (9–14), and lefty Mark Davis (5–17) contributed mightily to SF's last-in-the-league 4.39 team ERA.

The bullpen — righty Greg Minton (4–9, 19 saves) and lefty Gary Lavelle (5–4, 12 saves) — is in decent shape. But the starters never gave them much chance.

STAT LEADERS — 1984

BATTING
Average: C. Davis, .315
Runs: C. Davis, 87
Hits: C. Davis, 157
Doubles: Brenly, 28
Triples: C. Davis, 6
Home Runs: C. Davis, Leonard, 21
RBIs: Leonard, 86
Game-Winning RBIs: Leonard, 9
Stolen Bases: LeMaster, Leonard, 17

PITCHING
Wins: Krukow, 11
Losses: M. Davis, 17
Complete Games: Krukow, 3
Shutouts: Williams, Robinson, Krukow, 1
Saves: Minton, 19
Walks: Krukow, 78
Strikeouts: Krukow, 141

NL West
CINCINNATI REDS
1984 Finish: Fifth
1985 Prediction: Sixth

Pete Rose

Mario Soto

The best thing manager Pete Rose has going for him is player Pete Rose. Pete, also known as Charley Hustle, normally gives 110%. But with Ty Cobb's all-time base-hit record (4,191) just 94 hits away, Pete may crank it up to 120%

That should inspire the Reds, the team manager Rose took over last August 16. That inspired Rose, who hit better than .360 playing for himself, and even fired up sleeping SS Dave Concepcion (.245) and OF Cesar Cedeno (.276, but over .300 with Rose). Add Dave Parker (.285), the outstanding free-agent pickup and you have a solid nucleus.

Problem is, Rose can't pitch, and that's where he needs the most help. Don't fault Mario Soto, who worked 237+ innings and gave the bullpen plenty of free time, with a league-leading 13 complete games. He also won 18 (lost 7) for a 70–92 club. Ex-Met farmhand Jay Tibbs (6–2, 1.86) has the inside track on another starting spot. Righties Ron Robinson (1–2, 2.72) and Fred Tolliver (one earned run in 10 innings), and lefty Tom Browning (1–0, 1.54) all have excellent chances. Save leader Ted Power (9–7, 11 saves) improved greatly under Rose.

None of last year's infielders did much, though Wayne Krenchicki (.298) was adequate. The outfield was productive, with Parker leading the club in most categories. Gary Redus (.254) has plenty of speed and Cedeno is multitalented. Eric Davis, Kal Daniels, and Paul O'Neill could fit in.

Catching has been another Cincy weakness (where have you gone, Johnny Bench?). Look for Alan Knicely to get a shot at unseating Brad Gulden, Dave Van Gorder, and Dann Bilardello.

STAT LEADERS — 1984

BATTING

Average: Parker, .285
Runs: Parker, 73
Hits: Parker, 173
Doubles: Parker, 28
Triples: Esasky, 5
Home Runs: Parker, 16
RBIs: Parker, 94
Game-Winning RBIs: Parker, 13
Stolen Bases: Redus, 48

PITCHING

Wins: Soto, 18
Losses: Russell, 18*
Complete Games: Soto, 13*
Shutouts: Russell, 2
Saves: Power, 11
Walks: Soto, 87
Strikeouts: Soto, 185

*Led league.

Powerful Mike Schmidt, who shared NL home-run honors with 36 a year ago, is the key to the Phillies' efforts to bounce back.

STATISTICS
1984

AMERICAN LEAGUE
Batting
(80 or more at-bats)
*Bats Lefthanded   †Switch-Hitter

Batter and Club	AVG	G	AB	R	H	HR	RBI	SB
Aikens, Willie Tor.*	.205	93	234	21	48	11	26	0
Allenson, Gary, Bos.	.229	35	83	9	19	2	8	0
Almon, Bill, Oak.	.223	105	211	24	47	7	16	5
Armas, Tony, Bos.	.268	157	639	107	171	43	123	1
Ayala, Benny, Balt.	.212	60	118	9	25	4	24	1
Baines, Harold, Chi.*	.304	147	569	72	173	29	94	1
Baker, Doug, Det.†	.185	43	108	15	20	0	12	3
Balboni, Steve, K.C.	.244	126	438	58	107	28	77	0
Bando, Chris, Clev.†	.291	75	220	38	64	12	41	1
Bannister, Allan, Tex.	.295	47	112	20	33	2	9	3
Barfield, Jesse, Tor.	.284	110	320	51	91	14	49	8
Barrett, Marty, Bos.	.303	139	475	56	144	3	45	5
Baylor, Don, N.Y.	.262	134	493	84	129	27	89	1
Bell, Buddy, Tex.	.315	148	553	88	174	11	83	2
Bell, George, Tor.	.292	159	606	85	177	26	87	11
Beniquez, Juan, Cal.	.336	110	354	60	119	8	39	0
Bergman, Dave, Det.*	.273	120	271	42	74	7	44	3
Bernazard, Tony, Clev.†	.221	140	439	44	97	2	38	20
Biancalana, Buddy, K.C.†	.194	66	134	18	26	2	9	1
Bochte, Bruce, Oak.*	.264	148	469	58	124	5	52	2
Boggs, Wade, Bos.*	.325	158	625	109	203	6	55	3
Bonnell, Barry, Sea.	.264	110	363	42	96	8	48	5
Boone, Bob, Cal.	.202	139	450	33	91	3	32	3
Boston, Daryl, Chi.*	.169	35	83	8	14	0	3	6
Bradley, Phil, Sea.	.301	124	332	49	97	0	24	21
Brett, George, K.C.*	.284	104	377	42	107	13	69	0
Brookens, Tom, Det.	.246	113	224	32	55	5	26	6
Brouhard, Mark, Milw.	.239	66	197	20	47	6	22	0
Brown, Darrell, Minn.†	.273	95	260	36	71	1	19	4
Brown, Mike, Cal.	.284	62	148	19	42	7	22	0
Brunansky, Tom, Minn.	.254	155	567	75	144	32	85	4

Batter and Club	AVG	G	AB	R	H	HR	RBI	SB
Buckner, Bill, Bos.*	.278	114	439	51	122	11	67	2
Bumbry, Al, Balt.*	.270	119	344	47	93	3	24	9
Bush, Randy, Minn.*	.222	113	311	46	69	11	43	1
Butler, Brett, Clev.*	.269	159	602	108	162	3	49	52
Carew, Rod, Cal.*	.295	93	329	42	97	3	31	4
Carter, Joe, Clev.	.275	66	244	32	67	13	41	2
Castillo, Carmelo, Clev.	.261	87	211	36	55	10	36	1
Castillo, Marty, Det.	.234	70	141	16	33	4	17	1
Cerone, Rick, N.Y	.208	38	120	8	25	2	13	1
Clark, Bobby, Milw.	.260	58	169	17	44	2	16	1
Coles, Darnell, Sea.	.161	48	143	15	23	0	6	2
Collins, Dave, Tor.†	.308	128	441	59	136	2	44	60
Concepcion, Onix, K.C.	.282	90	287	36	81	1	23	9
Cooper, Cecil, Milw.*	.275	148	603	63	166	11	67	8
Cowens, Al, Sea.	.277	139	524	60	145	15	78	9
Cruz, Julio, Chi.†	.222	143	415	42	92	5	43	14
Cruz, Todd, Balt.	.218	96	142	15	31	3	9	1
Dauer, Rich, Balt.	.254	127	397	29	101	2	24	1
Davis, Alvin, Sea.*	.284	152	567	80	161	27	116	5
Davis, Butch, K.C.	.147	41	116	11	17	2	12	4
Davis, Mike, Oak.*	.230	134	382	47	88	9	46	14
Dayett, Brian, N.Y.	.244	64	127	14	31	4	23	0
DeCinces, Doug, Cal.	.269	146	547	77	147	20	82	4
Dempsey, Rick, Balt.	.230	109	330	37	76	11	34	1
Downing, Brian, Cal.	.275	156	539	65	148	23	91	0
Dwyer, Jim, Balt.*	.255	76	161	22	41	2	21	0
Dybzinski,Jerry, Chi.	.235	94	132	17	31	1	10	7
Easler, Mike, Bos.*	.313	156	601	87	188	27	91	1
Engle, Dave, Minn.	.266	109	391	56	104	4	38	0
Essian, Jim, Oak.	.235	63	136	17	32	2	10	1
Evans, Darrell, Det.*	.232	131	401	60	93	16	63	2
Evans, Dwight, Bos.	.295	162	630	121	186	32	104	3
Fernandez, Tony, Tor.†	.270	88	233	29	63	3	19	5
Fischlin, Mike, Clev.	.226	85	133	17	30	1	14	2
Fisk, Carlton, Chi.	.231	102	359	54	83	21	43	6
Fletcher, Scott, Chi.	.250	149	456	46	114	3	35	10
Foley, Marvis, Tex.*	.217	63	115	13	25	6	19	0

Batter and Club	AVG	G	AB	R	H	HR	RBI	SB
Foli, Tim, N.Y.	.252	61	163	8	41	0	16	0
Ford, Dan, Balt.	.231	25	91	7	21	1	5	1
Franco, Julio, Clev.	.286	160	658	82	188	3	79	19
Gaetti, Gary, Minn.	.262	162	588	55	154	5	65	11
Gamble, Oscar, N.Y.*	.184	54	125	17	23	10	27	1
Gantner, Jim, Milw.*	.282	153	613	61	173	3	56	6
Garbey, Barbaro, Det.	.287	110	327	45	94	5	52	6
Garcia, Damaso, Tor.	.284	152	633	79	180	5	46	46
Gedman, Rich, Bos.*	.269	133	449	54	121	24	72	0
Gibson, Kirk, Det.*	.282	149	531	92	150	27	91	29
Grich, Bobby, Cal.	.256	116	363	60	93	18	58	2
Griffey, Ken, N.Y.*	.273	120	399	44	109	7	56	2
Griffin, Alfredo, Tor.†	.241	140	419	53	101	4	30	11
Gross, Wayne, Balt.*	.216	127	342	53	74	22	64	1
Grubb, John, Det.*	.267	86	176	25	47	8	17	1
Gutierrez, Jackie, Bos.	.263	151	449	55	118	2	29	12
Hairston, Jerry, Chi.†	.260	115	227	41	59	5	19	2
Hall, Mel, Clev.*	.257	83	257	43	66	7	30	1
Hargrove, Mike, Clev.*	.267	133	352	44	94	2	44	0
Harrah, Toby, N.Y.	.217	88	253	40	55	1	26	3
Hassey, Ron, Clev.*	.255	48	149	11	38	0	19	1
Hatcher, Mickey, Minn.	.302	152	576	61	174	5	69	0
Heath, Mike, Oak.	.248	140	475	49	118	13	64	7
Henderson, Dave, Sea.	.280	112	350	42	98	14	43	5
Henderson, Rickey, Oak.	.293	142	502	113	147	16	58	66
Henderson, Steve, Sea.	.262	109	325	42	85	10	35	2
Herndon, Larry, Det.	.280	125	407	52	114	7	43	6
Hill, Donnie, Oak.†	.230	73	174	21	40	2	16	1
Hill, Marc, Chi.	.233	77	193	15	45	5	20	0
Hoffman, Glenn, Bos.	.189	64	74	8	14	0	4	0
Hostetler, Dave, Tex.	.220	37	82	7	18	3	10	0
Howell, Roy, Milw.*	.232	68	164	12	38	4	17	0
Hrbek, Kent, Minn.*	.311	149	559	80	174	27	107	1
Iorg, Dane, K.C.*	.255	78	235	27	60	5	30	0
Iorg, Garth, Tor.	.227	121	247	24	56	1	25	1
Jackson, Ron, Cal.-Balt.	.193	45	119	5	23	0	7	0
Jackson, Reggie, Cal.*	.223	143	525	67	117	25	81	8

Batter and Club	AVG	G	AB	R	H	HR	RBI	SB
Jacoby, Brook, Clev.	.264	126	439	64	116	7	40	3
James, Dion, Milw.*	.295	128	387	52	114	1	30	10
Jimenez, Houston, Minn.	.201	108	298	28	60	0	19	0
Johnson, Cliff, Tor.	.304	127	359	51	109	16	61	0
Johnson, Howard, Det.†	.248	116	355	43	88	12	50	10
Jones, Bobby, Tex.*	.259	64	143	14	37	4	22	1
Jones, Lynn, K.C.	.301	47	103	11	31	1	10	1
Jones, Ruppert, Det.*	.284	79	215	26	61	12	37	2
Kearney, Bob, Sea.	.225	133	431	39	97	7	43	7
Kemp, Steve, N.Y.*	.291	94	313	37	91	7	41	4
Kingman, Dave, Oak.	.268	147	549	68	147	35	118	2
Kittle, Ron, Chi.	.215	139	466	67	100	32	74	3
Kunkel, Jeff, Tex.	.204	50	142	13	29	3	7	4
Kuntz, Rusty, Det.	.286	84	140	32	40	2	22	2
Lansford, Carney, Oak.	.300	151	597	70	179	14	74	9
Laudner, Tim, Minn.	.206	87	262	31	54	10	35	0
Law, Rudy, Chi.	.251	136	487	68	122	6	37	29
Law, Vance, Chi.	.252	151	481	60	121	17	59	4
Leach, Rick, Tor.*	.261	65	88	11	23	0	7	0
Lemon, Chet, Det.	.287	141	509	77	146	20	76	5
Lopes, Davey, Oak.	.257	72	230	32	59	9	36	12
Lowenstein, John, Balt.*	.237	105	270	34	64	8	28	1
Lozado, Willie, Milw.	.271	43	107	15	29	1	20	0
Luzinski, Greg, Chi.	.238	125	412	47	98	13	58	5
Lynn, Fred, Cal.*	.271	142	517	84	140	23	79	2
Manning, Rick, Milw.*	.249	119	341	53	85	7	31	5
Martinez, Buck, Tor.	.220	102	232	24	51	5	37	0
Mattingly, Don, N.Y.*	.343	153	603	91	207	23	110	1
McRae, Hal, K.C.	.303	106	317	30	96	3	42	0
Meacham, Bobby, N.Y.†	.253	99	360	62	91	2	25	9
Meier, Dave, Minn.	.238	59	147	18	35	0	13	0
Milbourne, Larry, Sea.†	.265	79	211	22	56	1	22	0
Miller, Rick, Bos.†	.260	95	123	17	32	0	12	1
Moore, Charlie, Milw.	.234	70	188	13	44	2	17	0
Moreno, Omar, N.Y.*	.259	117	355	37	92	4	38	20
Morgan, Joe, Oak.*	.244	116	365	50	89	6	43	8
Moseby, Lloyd, Tor.*	.280	158	592	97	166	18	92	39

Batter and Club	AVG	G	AB	R	H	HR	RBI	SB
Motley, Darryl, K.C.	.284	146	522	64	148	15	70	10
Mulliniks, Rance, Tor.*	.324	125	343	41	111	3	42	2
Murphy, Dwayne, Oak.*	.256	153	559	93	143	33	88	4
Murray, Eddie, Balt.†	.306	162	588	97	180	29	110	10
Narron, Jerry, Cal.*	.247	69	150	9	37	3	17	0
Nichols, Reid, Bos.	.226	74	124	14	28	1	14	2
Nixon, Otis, Clev.†	.154	49	91	16	14	0	1	12
Obrien, Pete, Tex.*	.287	142	520	57	149	18	80	3
Oglivie, Ben, Milw.*	.262	131	461	49	121	12	60	0
Orta, Jorge, K.C.*	.298	122	403	50	120	9	50	0
Owen, Spike, Sea.†	.245	152	530	67	130	3	43	16
Paciorek, Tom, Chi.	.256	111	363	35	93	4	29	6
Pagliarulo, Mike, N.Y.	.239	67	201	24	48	7	34	0
Parrish, Lance, Det.	.237	147	578	75	137	33	98	2
Parrish, Larry, Tex.	.285	156	613	72	175	22	101	2
Perconte, Jack, Sea.*	.294	155	612	93	180	0	31	29
Perkins, Broderick, Clev.*	.197	58	66	5	13	0	4	0
Pettis, Gary, Cal.†	.227	140	397	63	90	2	29	48
Phelps, Ken, Sea.	.241	101	290	52	70	24	51	3
Phillips, Tony, Oak.†	.266	154	451	62	120	4	37	10
Picciolo, Rob, Cal.	.202	87	119	18	24	1	9	0
Piniella, Lou, N.Y.	.302	29	86	8	26	1	6	0
Presley, Jim, Sea.	.227	70	251	27	57	10	36	1
Pryor, Greg, K.C.	.263	123	270	32	71	4	25	0
Puckett, Kirby, Minn.	.296	128	557	63	165	0	31	14
Putnam, Pat, Sea.-Minn.*	.176	78	193	12	34	2	20	3
Ramos, Domingo, Sea.	.185	59	81	6	15	0	2	2
Randolph, Willie, N.Y.	.287	142	564	86	162	2	31	10
Rayford, Floyd, Balt.	.256	86	250	24	64	4	27	0
Ready, Randy, Milw.	.187	37	123	13	23	3	13	0
Remy, Jerry, Bos.*	.250	30	104	8	26	0	8	4
Rice, Jim, Bos.	.280	159	657	98	184	28	122	4
Ripken, Cal, Balt.	.304	162	641	103	195	27	86	2
Rivers, Mickey, Tex.*	.300	102	313	40	94	4	33	5
Robertson, Andre, N.Y.	.214	52	140	10	30	0	6	0
Roenicke, Gary, Balt.	.224	121	326	36	73	10	44	1
Romero, Ed, Milw.	.252	116	357	36	90	1	31	3

Batter and Club	AVG	G	AB	R	H	HR	RBI	SB
Sakata, Lenn, Balt.	.191	81	157	23	30	3	11	4
Sample, Billy, Tex.	.247	130	489	67	121	5	33	18
Schofield, Dick, Cal.	.193	140	400	39	77	4	21	5
Schroeder, Bill, Milw.	.257	61	210	29	54	14	25	0
Sconiers, Daryl, Cal.*	.244	57	160	14	39	4	17	1
Scott, Donnie, Tex.†	.221	81	235	16	52	3	20	0
Shelby, John, Balt.†	.209	128	383	44	80	6	30	12
Sheridan, Pat, K.C.*	.283	138	481	64	136	8	53	19
Simmons, Ted, Milw.†	.221	132	497	44	110	4	52	3
Singleton, Ken, Balt.†	.215	111	363	28	78	6	36	0
Skinner, Joel, Chi.	.213	43	80	4	17	0	3	1
Slaught, Don, K.C.	.264	124	409	48	108	4	42	0
Smalley, Roy, N.Y.-Chi.†	.212	114	344	32	73	11	39	3
Squires, Mike, Chi.*	.183	104	82	9	15	0	6	2
Stegman, Dave, Chi.	.261	55	92	13	24	2	11	3
Sundberg, Jim, Milw.	.261	110	348	43	91	7	43	1
Tabler, Pat, Clev.	.290	144	473	66	137	10	68	3
Teufel, Tim, Minn.	.262	157	568	76	149	14	61	1
Thomas, Gorman, Sea.	.157	35	108	6	17	1	13	0
Thornton, Andre, Clev.	.271	155	587	91	159	33	99	6
Tolleson, Wayne, Tex.†	.213	118	338	35	72	0	9	22
Trammell, Alan, Det.	.314	139	555	85	174	14	69	19
Upshaw, Willie, Tor.*	.278	152	569	79	158	19	84	10
Vukovich, George, Clev.*	.304	134	437	38	133	9	60	1
Wagner, Mark, Oak.	.230	83	87	8	20	0	12	2
Walker, Greg, Chi.*	.294	136	442	62	130	24	75	8
Ward, Gary, Tex.	.284	155	602	97	171	21	79	7
Washington, Ron, Minn.	.294	88	197	25	58	3	23	1
Washington, U.L., K.C.†	.224	63	170	18	38	1	10	4
Wathan, John, K.C.	.181	97	171	17	31	2	10	6
Whitaker, Lou, Det.*	.289	143	558	90	161	13	56	6
White, Frank, K.C.	.271	129	479	58	130	17	56	5
Whitt, Ernie, Tor.*	.238	124	315	35	75	15	46	0
Wilfong, Rob, Cal.*	.248	108	307	31	76	6	33	3
Wilkerson, Curtis, Tex.†	.248	153	484	47	120	1	26	12
Willard, Jerry, Clev.*	.224	87	246	21	55	10	37	1
Wilson, Willie, K.C.†	.301	128	541	81	163	2	44	47

Batter and Club	AVG	G	AB	R	H	HR	RBI	SB
Winfield, Dave, N.Y.........	.340	141	567	106	193	19	100	6
Wright, George, Tex.†	.243	101	383	40	93	9	48	0
Wynegar, Butch, N.Y.†......	.267	129	442	48	118	6	45	1
Yost, Ned, Tex...............	.182	80	242	15	44	6	25	1
Young, Mike, Balt.†	.252	123	401	59	101	17	52	6
Yount, Robin, Milw.	.298	160	624	105	186	16	80	14

AMERICAN LEAGUE

Pitching

(80 or more innings pitched)
*Throws Lefthanded

Pitcher and Club	W	L	ERA	G	IP	H	BB	SO
Alexander, Doyle, Tor.	17	6	3.13	36	261.2	238	59	139
Atherton, Keith, Oak.	7	6	4.33	57	104.0	110	39	58
Bair, Doug, Det.	5	3	3.75	47	93.2	82	36	57
Bannister, Floyd, Chi.*	14	11	4.83	34	218.0	211	80	152
Barojas, S., Chi.-Sea.	9	7	4.14	43	134.2	136	60	55
Beattie, Jim, Sea.	12	16	3.41	32	211.0	206	75	119
Beckwith, Joe, K.C.	8	4	3.40	49	100.2	92	25	75
Berenguer, Juan, Det.......	11	10	3.48	31	168.1	146	79	118
Black, Bud, K.C.*	17	12	3.12	35	257.0	226	64	140
Blyleven, Bert, Clev.........	19	7	2.87	33	245.0	204	74	170
Boddicker, Mike, Balt.	20	11	2.79	34	261.1	218	81	128
Boyd, Dennis, Bos.	12	12	4.37	29	197.2	207	53	134
Burns, Britt, Chi.*	4	12	5.00	34	117.0	130	45	85
Burris, Ray, Oak.	13	10	3.15	34	211.2	193	90	93
Butcher, John, Minn.	13	11	3.44	34	225.0	242	53	83
Caldwell, Mike, Milw.*.....	6	13	4.64	26	126.0	160	21	34
Camacho, Ernie, Clev.	5	9	2.43	69	100.0	83	37	48
Caudill, Bill, Oak............	9	7	2.71	68	96.1	77	31	89
Clancy, Jim, Tor.............	13	15	5.12	36	219.2	249	88	118
Clemens, Roger, Bos.......	9	4	4.32	21	133.1	146	29	126
Cocanower, Jaime, Milw...	8	16	4.02	33	174.2	188	78	65
Codiroli, Chris, Oak.......	6	4	5.84	28	89.1	111	34	44
Comer, Steve, Clev.	4	8	5.68	22	117.1	146	39	39
Conroy, Tim, Oak.*	1	6	5.23	38	93.0	82	63	69
Corbett, Doug, Cal.	5	1	2.12	45	85.0	76	30	48
Cowley, Joe, N.Y............	9	2	3.56	16	83.1	75	31	71
Darwin, Danny, Tex.	8	12	3.94	35	223.2	249	54	123
Davis, Ron, Minn.	7	11	4.55	64	83.0	79	41	74
Davis, Storm, Balt.	14	9	3.12	35	225.0	205	71	105
Dotson, Richard, Chi.	14	15	3.59	32	245.2	216	103	120
Farr, Steve, Clev.	3	11	4.58	31	116.0	106	46	83

Pitcher and Club	W	L	ERA	G	IP	H	BB	SO
Filson, Pete, Minn.*	6	5	4.10	55	118.2	106	54	59
Flanagan, Mike, Balt.*	13	13	3.53	34	226.2	213	81	115
Fontenot, Ray, N.Y.*	8	9	3.61	35	169.1	189	58	85
Gott, Jim, Tor.	7	6	4.02	35	109.2	93	49	73
Gubicza, Mark, K.C.	10	14	4.05	29	189.0	172	75	111
Guidry, Ron, N.Y.*	10	11	4.51	29	195.2	223	44	127
Gura, Larry, K.C.*	12	9	5.18	31	168.2	175	67	68
Haas, Moose, Milw.	9	11	3.99	31	189.1	205	43	84
Heaton, Neal, Clev.*	12	15	5.21	38	198.2	231	75	75
Hernandez, Willie, Det.*	9	3	1.92	80	140.1	96	36	112
Hodge, Ed, Minn.	4	3	4.77	25	100.0	116	29	59
Hough, Charlie, Tex.	16	14	3.76	36	266.0	260	94	164
Howell, Jay, N.Y.	9	4	2.69	61	103.2	86	34	109
Hoyt, LaMarr, Chi.	13	18	4.47	34	235.2	244	43	126
Hurst, Bruce, Bos.*	12	12	3.92	33	218.0	232	88	136
Jackson, Roy Lee, Tor.	7	8	3.56	54	86.0	73	31	58
John, Tommy, Cal.*	7	13	4.52	32	181.1	223	56	47
Jones, Mike, K.C.*	2	3	4.89	23	81.0	86	36	43
Krueger, Bill, Oak.*	10	10	4.75	26	142.0	156	85	61
Ladd, Pete, Milw.	4	9	5.24	54	91.0	94	38	75
Lamp, Dennis, Tor.	8	8	4.55	56	85.0	97	38	45
Langston, Mark, Sea.*	17	10	3.40	35	225.0	188	118	204
Leal, Luis, Tor.	13	8	3.89	35	222.1	221	77	134
Leibrandt, Charlie, K.C.*	11	7	3.63	23	143.2	158	38	53
Lopez, Aurelio, Det.	10	1	2.94	71	137.2	109	52	94
Martinez, Dennis, Balt.	6	9	5.02	34	141.2	145	37	77
Martinez, Tippy, Balt.*	4	9	3.91	55	89.2	88	51	72
Mason, Mike, Tex.*	9	13	3.61	36	184.1	159	51	113
McCatty, Steve, Oak.	8	14	4.76	33	179.2	206	71	63
McClure, Bob, Milw.*	4	8	4.38	39	139.2	154	52	68
McGregor, Scott, Balt.*	15	12	3.94	30	196.1	216	54	67
Moore, Mike, Sea.	7	17	4.97	34	212.0	236	85	158
Morris, Jack, Det.	19	11	3.60	35	240.1	221	87	148
Niekro, Phil, N.Y.	16	8	3.09	32	215.2	219	76	136
Nipper, Al, Bos.	11	6	3.89	29	182.2	183	52	84
Ojeda, Bob, Bos.*	12	12	3.99	33	216.2	211	96	137
Petry, Dan, Det.	18	8	3.24	35	233.1	231	66	144

Pitcher and Club	W	L	ERA	G	IP	H	BB	SO
Porter, Chuck, Milw.	6	4	3.87	17	81.1	92	12	48
Rasmussen, D., N.Y.*.....	9	6	4.57	24	147.2	127	60	110
Righetti, Dave, N.Y.	5	6	2.34	64	96.1	79	37	90
Romanick, Ron, Cal.	12	12	3.76	33	229.2	240	61	87
Rozema, Dave, Det.	7	6	3.74	29	101.0	110	18	48
Saberhagen, Bret, K.C.	10	11	3.48	38	157.2	138	36	73
Sanchez, Luis, Cal.	9	7	3.33	49	83.2	84	33	62
Schrom, Ken, Minn.	5	11	4.47	25	137.0	156	41	49
Schulze, Don, Clev.	3	6	4.83	19	85.2	105	27	39
Seaver, Tom, Chi.	15	11	3.95	34	236.2	216	61	131
Shirley, Bob, N.Y.*	3	3	3.38	41	114.1	119	38	48
Slaton, Jim, Cal.	7	10	4.97	32	163.0	192	56	67
Smith, Leroy, Clev.	5	5	4.59	22	86.1	91	40	55
Smithson, Mike, Minn.....	15	13	3.68	36	252.0	246	54	144
Sorensen, Lary, Oak.	6	13	4.91	46	183.1	240	44	63
Spillner, Dan, Clev.-Chi. ...	1	5	4.89	36	99.1	121	36	49
Stanley, Bob, Bos.	9	10	3.54	57	106.2	113	23	52
Stewart, Dave, Tex.	7	14	4.73	32	192.1	193	87	119
Stewart, Sammy, Balt......	7	4	3.29	60	93.0	81	47	56
Stieb, Dave, Tor.	16	8	2.83	35	267.0	215	88	198
Sutcliffe, Rick, Clev.	4	5	5.15	15	94.1	111	46	58
Sutton, Don, Milw.	14	12	3.77	33	212.2	224	51	143
Tanana, Frank, Tex.*	15	15	3.25	35	246.1	234	81	141
Tellmann, Tom, Milw.	6	3	2.78	50	81.0	82	31	28
Vande Berg, Ed, Sea.*.....	8	12	4.76	50	130.1	165	50	71
Viola, Frank, Minn.*	18	12	3.21	35	257.2	225	73	149
Waddell, Tom, Clev.	7	4	3.06	58	97.0	68	37	59
Warren, Mike, Oak.	3	6	4.90	24	90.0	104	44	61
Wilcox, Milt, Det.	17	8	4.00	33	193.2	183	66	119
Witt, Mike, Cal.	15	11	3.47	34	246.2	227	84	196
Young, Curt, Oak.*	9	4	4.06	20	108.2	118	31	41
Young, Matt, Sea.*	6	8	5.72	22	113.1	141	57	73
Zahn, Geoff, Cal.*	13	10	3.12	28	199.1	200	48	61

NATIONAL LEAGUE
Batting
(60 or more at-bats)
*Bats Lefthanded †Switch-Hitter

Batter and Club	AVG	G	AB	R	H	HR	RBI	SB
Aguayo, Louis, Phil.	.278	58	72	15	20	3	11	0
Anderson, David, L.A.	.251	121	374	51	94	3	34	15
Andujar, Joaquin, St.L.†	.131	36	84	8	11	2	8	1
Ashby, Alan, Hou.†	.262	66	191	16	50	4	27	0
Backman, Walter, N.Y.†	.280	128	436	68	122	1	26	32
Bailey, J. Mark, Hou.†	.212	108	344	38	73	9	34	0
Bailor, Robert, L.A.	.275	65	131	11	36	0	8	3
Baker, Johnnie, S.F.	.292	100	243	31	71	3	32	4
Bass, Kevin, Hou.†	.260	121	331	33	86	2	29	5
Benedict, Bruce, Atl.	.223	95	300	26	67	4	25	1
Berra, Dale, Pitt.	.222	136	450	31	100	9	52	1
Bevacqua, Kurt, S.D.	.200	59	80	7	16	1	9	0
Bilardello, Dann, Cin.	.209	68	182	16	38	2	10	0
Bochy, Bruce, S.D.	.228	37	92	10	21	4	15	0
Bosley, Thaddis, Chi.*	.296	55	98	17	29	2	14	5
Bowa, Lawrence, Chi.†	.223	133	391	33	87	0	17	10
Braun, Stephen, St.L.*	.276	86	98	6	27	0	16	0
Brenly, Robert, S.F.	.291	145	506	74	147	20	80	6
Brock, Gregory, L.A.*	.225	88	271	33	61	14	34	8
Brooks, Hubert, N.Y.	.283	153	561	61	159	16	73	6
Brown, J. Chris., S.F.	.286	23	84	6	24	1	11	2
Brown, Rogers, S.D.†	.251	85	171	28	43	3	29	16
Cabell, Enos, Hou.	.310	127	436	52	135	8	44	8
Candelaria, John, Pitt.†	.129	33	62	6	8	1	2	0
Carlton, Steven, Phil.*	.190	34	84	8	16	1	10	0
Carter, Gary, Mtl.	.294	159	596	75	175	27	106	2
Cedeno, Cesar, Cin.	.276	110	380	59	105	10	47	19
Cey, Ronald, Chi.	.240	146	505	71	121	25	97	3
Chambliss, Chris., Atl.*	.257	135	389	47	100	9	44	1
Chapman, Kelvin, N.Y.	.289	75	197	27	57	3	23	8
Clark, Jack, S.F.	.320	57	203	33	65	11	44	1

Batter and Club	AVG	G	AB	R	H	HR	RBI	SB
Concepcion, David, Cin.....	.245	154	531	46	130	4	58	22
Corcoran, Timothy, Phil.*	.341	102	208	30	71	5	36	0
Cotto, Henry, Chi.	.274	105	146	24	40	0	8	9
Cruz, Jose, Hou.*	.312	160	600	96	187	12	95	22
Darling, Ronald, N.Y.	.149	39	67	7	10	0	3	0
Davis, Charles, S.F.†	.315	137	499	87	157	21	81	12
Davis, Eric, Cin.	.224	57	174	33	39	10	30	10
Davis, Glenn, Hou.	.213	18	61	6	13	2	8	0
Davis, Jody, Chi.	.256	150	523	55	134	19	94	5
Dawson, Andre, Mtl.	.248	138	533	73	132	17	86	13
DeJesus, Ivan, Phil.	.257	144	435	40	112	0	35	12
Dernier, Robert, Chi.	.278	143	536	94	149	3	32	45
Diaz, Baudilio, Phil.	.213	27	75	5	16	1	9	0
Dilone, Miguel, Mtl.†	.278	88	169	28	47	1	10	27
Distefano, Benito, Pitt.* ..	.167	45	78	10	13	3	9	0
Doran, William, Hou.†	.261	147	548	92	143	4	41	21
Driessen, D., Cin.-Mtl.*	.269	132	387	47	104	16	60	2
Durham, Leon, Chi.*	.279	137	473	86	132	23	96	16
Esasky, Nicholas, Cin.	.193	113	322	30	62	10	45	1
Fitzgerald, Michael, N.Y.	.242	112	360	20	87	2	33	1
Flannery, Timothy, S.D.* ..	.273	86	128	24	35	2	10	4
Flynn, R. Douglas, Mtl......	.243	124	366	23	89	0	17	0
Foley, Thomas, Cin.*	.253	106	277	26	70	5	27	3
Foster, George, N.Y.	.269	146	553	67	149	24	86	2
Francona, Terry, Mtl.*	.346	58	214	18	74	1	18	0
Frobel, Douglas, Pitt.*	.203	126	276	33	56	12	28	7
Garcia, Alfonso, Phil.	.233	57	60	6	14	0	5	0
Gardenhire, Ronald, N.Y. ...	.246	74	207	20	51	1	10	6
Garner, Philip, Hou.	.278	128	374	60	104	4	45	3
Garvey, Steven, S.D.........	.284	161	617	72	175	8	86	1
Gladden, C. Daniel, S.F.....	.351	86	342	71	120	4	31	31
Gonzalez, Denio, Pitt.......	.183	26	82	9	15	0	4	1
Gooden, Dwight, N.Y...:....	.200	31	70	5	14	0	3	0
Green, David, St.L.	.268	126	452	49	121	15	65	17
Gross, Gregory, Phil.*	.322	112	202	19	65	0	16	1
Guerrero, Pedro, L.A........	.303	144	535	85	162	16	72	9
Gulden, Bradley, Cin.*	.226	107	292	31	66	4	33	2

Batter and Club	AVG	G	AB	R	H	HR	RBI	SB
Gullickson, William, Mtl.	.110	32	73	1	8	0	1	0
Gwynn, Anthony, S.D.*	.351	158	606	88	213	5	71	33
Hall, Albert, Atl.†	.261	87	142	25	37	1	9	6
Hall, Melvin, Chi.*	.280	48	150	25	42	4	22	2
Harper, Brian, Pitt.	.259	46	112	4	29	2	11	0
Harper, Terry, Atl.	.157	40	102	4	16	0	8	4
Hayes, Von, Phil.*	.292	152	561	85	164	16	67	48
Hebner, Richard, Chi.*	.333	44	81	12	27	2	8	1
Heep, Daniel, N.Y.*	.231	99	199	36	46	1	12	3
Hendrick, George, St.L.	.277	120	441	57	122	9	69	0
Hernandez, Keith, N.Y.*	.311	154	550	83	171	15	94	2
Herr, Thomas, St.L.†	.276	145	558	67	154	4	49	13
Hodges, Ronald, N.Y.*	.208	64	106	5	22	1	11	1
Horner, J. Robert, Atl.	.274	32	113	15	31	3	19	0
Howe, Arthur, St.L.	.216	89	139	17	30	2	12	0
Hubbard, Glenn, Atl.	.234	120	397	53	93	9	43	4
Jeltz, L. Steven, Phil.	.206	28	68	7	14	1	7	2
Johnson, Randall, Atl.	.279	91	294	28	82	5	30	4
Johnstone, John, Chi.*	.288	52	73	8	21	0	3	0
Jorgensen, M., Atl.-St.L.*	.250	90	124	9	31	1	17	0
Kennedy, Terrence, S.D.*	.240	148	530	54	127	14	57	1
Knepper, Robert, Hou.*	.171	35	76	6	13	1	8	1
Knight, C. Ray, Hou.-N.Y.	.237	115	371	28	88	3	35	0
Komminsk, Brad, Atl.	.203	90	301	37	61	8	36	18
Koosman, Jerry, Phil.	.108	36	74	2	8	0	3	0
Krenchicki, Wayne, Cin.*	.298	97	181	18	54	6	22	0
Krukow, Michael, S.F.	.139	36	72	5	10	0	2	0
Kuiper, Duane, S.F.*	.200	83	115	8	23	0	11	0
Lacy, Leondaus, Pitt.	.321	138	474	66	152	12	70	21
Landreaux, Ken., L.A.*	.251	134	438	39	110	11	47	10
Landrum, Terry, St.L	.272	105	173	21	47	3	26	3
Laskey, William, S.F.	.063	35	63	3	4	0	0	0
Lawless, T., Cin.-Mtl.	.237	54	97	11	23	1	2	7
Lea, Charles, Mtl.	.111	30	72	3	8	0	0	0
Lefebvre, Joseph, Phil.*	.250	52	160	22	40	3	18	0
LeMaster, Johnnie, S.F.	.217	132	451	46	98	4	32	17
Leonard, Jeffrey, S.F.	.302	136	514	76	155	21	86	17

Batter and Club	AVG	G	AB	R	H	HR	RBI	SB
Lezcano, Sixto, Phil.	.277	109	256	36	71	14	40	0
Little, R. Bryan, Mtl.†	.244	85	266	31	65	0	9	2
Lollar, W. Timothy, S.D.*	.221	31	68	6	15	3	15	0
Lyons, William, St.L.	.219	46	73	13	16	0	3	3
Maddox, Garry, Phil.	.282	77	241	29	68	5	19	3
Madlock, Bill, Pitt.	.253	103	403	38	102	4	44	3
Mahler, Richard, Atl.	.296	38	71	6	21	0	3	0
Maldonado, Candido, L.A.	.268	116	254	25	68	5	28	0
Marshall, Michael, L.A.	.257	134	495	68	127	21	65	4
Martin, Jerry, N.Y.	.154	51	91	6	14	3	5	0
Martinez, Carmelo, S.D.	.250	149	488	64	122	13	66	1
Matthews, Gary, Chi.	.291	147	491	101	143	14	82	17
Matuszek, Leonard, Phil.*	.248	101	262	40	65	12	43	4
May, Milton, Pitt.*	.177	50	96	4	17	1	8	0
Mazzilli, Lee, Pitt.†	.237	111	266	37	63	4	21	8
McGee, Willie, St.L.†	.291	145	571	82	166	6	50	43
McReynolds, W.K., S.D.	.278	147	525	68	146	20	75	3
McWilliams, Larry, Pitt.*	.122	36	74	1	9	0	4	0
Milner, Eddie, Cin.*	.232	117	336	44	78	7	29	21
Moreland, B. Keith, Chi.	.279	140	495	59	138	16	80	1
Morrison, James, Pitt.	.286	100	304	38	87	11	45	0
Mullins, Francis, S.F.	.218	57	110	8	24	2	10	3
Mumphrey, Jerry, Hou.†	.290	151	524	66	152	9	83	15
Murphy, Dale, Atl.	.290	162	607	94	176	36	100	19
Nettles, Graig, S.D.*	.228	124	395	56	90	20	65	0
Nicosia, Steven, S.F.	.303	48	132	9	40	2	19	1
Niekro, Joseph, Hou.	.133	38	83	4	11	0	6	0
Nieto, Thomas, St.L.	.279	33	86	7	24	3	12	0
Oberkfell, K., St.L.-Atl.*	.269	100	324	38	87	1	21	2
Oester, Ronald, Cin.†	.242	150	553	54	134	3	38	7
Oliver, Albert, S.F.-Phil.*	.301	119	432	36	130	0	48	3
Oquendo, Jose, N.Y.	.222	81	189	23	42	0	10	10
Orsulak, Joseph, Pitt.*	.254	32	67	12	17	0	3	3
Ortiz, Adalberto, N.Y.	.198	40	91	6	18	0	11	1
Otis, Amos, Pitt.	.165	40	97	6	16	0	10	0
Owen, Dave, Chi.†	.194	47	93	8	18	1	10	1
Pankovits, James, Hou.	.284	53	81	6	23	1	14	2

Batter and Club	AVG	G	AB	R	H	HR	RBI	SB
Parker, David, Cin.*	.285	156	607	73	173	16	94	11
Pena, Alejandro, L.A.	.121	28	66	5	8	0	1	0
Pena, Antonio, Pitt.	.286	147	546	77	156	15	78	12
Pendleton, Terry, St.L.†	.324	67	262	37	85	1	33	20
Perez, Atanasio, Cin.	.241	71	137	9	33	2	15	0
Perez, Pascual, Atl.	.076	32	66	5	5	0	3	1
Perry, Gerald, Atl.*	.265	122	347	52	92	7	47	15
Porter, Darrell, St.L.*	.232	127	422	56	98	11	68	5
Puhl, Terrance, Hou.*	.301	132	449	66	135	9	55	13
Rabb, John, S.F.	.195	54	82	10	16	3	9	1
Raines, Timothy, Mtl.†	.309	160	622	106	192	8	60	75
Ramirez, Rafael, Atl.	.266	145	591	51	157	2	48	14
Ramos, Roberto, Mtl.	.193	31	83	8	16	2	5	0
Ramsey, M., St.L.-Mtl.†	.188	58	85	3	16	0	3	0
Ray, Johnny, Pitt.†	.312	155	555	75	173	6	67	11
Redus, Gary, Cin	.254	123	394	69	100	7	22	48
Reynolds, G. Craig, Hou.*	.260	146	527	61	137	6	60	7
Reynolds, Robert, L.A.†	.258	73	240	24	62	2	24	7
Rhoden, Richard, Pitt.	.333	35	84	9	28	0	4	0
Richards, Eugene, S.F.*	.252	87	135	18	34	0	4	5
Rivera, German, L.A.	.260	94	227	20	59	2	17	1
Robinson, Jeffrey, S.F.	.115	34	61	0	7	0	2	0
Rose, Peter, Mtl.-Cin.†	.286	121	374	43	107	0	34	1
Royster, Jeron, Atl.	.207	81	227	22	47	1	21	6
Runge, Paul, Atl.	.267	28	90	5	24	0	3	5
Russell, John, Phil.	.283	39	99	11	28	2	11	0
Russell, William, L.A.	.267	89	262	25	70	0	19	4
Ryan, L. Nolan, Hou.	.098	30	61	3	6	0	1	1
Salazar, Argenis, Mtl.	.155	80	174	12	27	0	12	1
Salazar, Louis, S.D.	.241	93	228	20	55	3	17	11
Samuel, Juan, Phil.	.272	160	701	105	191	15	69	72
Sandberg, Ryne, Chi.	.314	156	636	114	200	19	84	32
Santana, Rafael, N.Y.	.276	51	152	14	42	1	12	0
Sax, Stephen, L.A.	.243	145	569	70	138	1	35	34
Schmidt, Michael, Phil.	.277	151	528	93	146	36	106	5
Scioscia, Michael, L.A.*	.273	114	341	29	93	5	38	2
Scott, A., Hou.-Mtl.†	.239	70	92	10	22	0	5	1

Batter and Club	AVG	G	AB	R	H	HR	RBI	SB
Show, Eric, S.D.	.246	32	69	7	17	3	10	0
Smith, Lonnie, St.L.	.250	145	504	77	126	6	49	50
Smith, Osborne, St.L.†	.257	124	412	53	106	1	44	35
Soto, Mario, Cin.	.207	33	87	5	18	1	9	0
Speier, Chris, Mtl.-St.L.	.171	63	158	10	27	3	9	0
Spilman, W. Harry, Hou.*	.264	32	72	14	19	2	15	0
Staub, Daniel, N.Y.*	.264	78	72	2	19	1	18	0
Stenhouse, Michael, Mtl.*	.183	80	175	14	32	4	16	0
Stone, Jeffery, Phil.*	.362	51	185	27	67	1	15	27
Strawberry, Darryl, N.Y.*	.251	147	522	75	131	26	97	27
Stubbs, Franklin, L.A.*	.194	87	217	22	42	8	17	2
Templeton, Garry, S.D.†	.258	148	493	40	127	2	35	8
Terrell, C. Walter, N.Y.*	.080	33	75	3	6	0	0	0
Thomas, Derrel, Mtl.†	.255	108	243	26	62	0	20	0
Thompson, Jason, Pitt.*	.254	154	543	61	138	17	74	0
Thompson, Milton Atl.*	.303	25	99	16	30	2	4	14
Thompson, V. Scot, S.F.*	.306	120	245	30	75	1	31	5
Trevino, A., Cin.-Atl.	.243	85	272	36	66	3	28	5
Trillo, J. Manuel, S.F.	.254	98	401	45	102	4	36	0
Trout, Steven, Chi.*	.131	32	61	4	8	0	3	0
Tudor, John, Pitt.*	.211	36	76	3	16	0	2	1
Valenzuela, F., L.A.*	.190	35	79	5	15	3	7	0
Van Gorder, David, Cin.	.228	38	101	10	23	0	6	0
Van Slyke, Andrew, St.L.*	.244	137	361	45	88	7	50	28
Venable, W.M., Mtl.*	.239	38	71	7	17	2	7	1
Veryzer, Thomas, Chi.	.189	44	74	5	14	0	4	0
Virgil, Osvaldo, Phil.	.261	141	456	61	119	18	68	1
Walker, Duane, Cin.*	.292	83	195	35	57	10	28	7
Wallach, Timothy, Mtl.	.246	160	582	55	143	18	72	3
Walling, Dennis, Hou.*	.281	87	249	37	70	3	31	7
Washington, C., Atl.*	.286	120	416	62	119	17	61	21
Watson, Robert, Atl.	.212	49	85	4	18	2	12	0
Wellman, Brad, S.F.	.226	93	265	23	60	2	25	10
Whitfield, Terry, L.A.*	.244	87	180	15	44	4	18	1
Whitson, Eddie, S.D.	.049	36	61	0	3	0	1	0
Wiggins, Alan, S.D.†	.258	158	596	106	154	3	34	70
Wilson, Glenn, Phil.	.240	132	341	28	82	6	31	7

Batter and Club	AVG	G	AB	R	H	HR	RBI	SB
Wilson, William, N.Y.†	.276	154	587	88	162	10	54	46
Wockenfuss, John, Phil.	.289	86	180	20	52	6	24	1
Wohlford, James, Mtl.	.300	95	213	20	64	5	29	3
Woods, Gary, Chi.	.235	87	98	13	23	3	10	2
Wynne, Marvell, Pitt.*	.266	154	653	77	174	0	39	24
Yeager, Stephen, L.A.	.228	74	197	16	45	4	29	1
Youngblood, Joel, S.F.	.254	134	469	50	119	10	51	5

NATIONAL LEAGUE
Pitching
(60 or more innings pitched)
*Throws Lefthanded

Pitcher and Club	W	L	ERA	G	IP	H	BB	SO
Allen, Neil, St.L.	9	6	3.55	57	119.0	105	49	66
Andersen, Larry, Phil.	3	7	2.38	64	90.2	85	25	54
Andujar, Joaquin, St.L.	20	14	3.34	36	261.1	218	70	147
Barker, Leonard, Atl.	7	8	3.85	21	126.1	120	38	95
Bedrosian, Stephen, Atl. ..	9	6	2.37	40	83.2	65	33	81
Berenyi, B., Cin.-N.Y.	12	13	4.45	32	166.0	163	95	134
Bordi, Richard, Chi..........	5	2	3.46	31	83.1	78	20	41
Brusstar, Warren, Chi......	1	1	3.11	41	63.2	57	21	36
Camp, Rick, Atl.............	8	6	3.27	31	148.2	134	63	69
Campbell, William, Phil. ..	6	5	3.43	57	81.1	68	35	52
Candelaria, John, Pitt.* ...	12	11	2.72	33	185.1	179	34	133
Carlton, Steven, Phil.*	13	7	3.58	33	229.0	214	79	163
Cox, Danny, St.L.	9	11	4.03	29	156.1	171	54	70
Darling, Ronald, N.Y.	12	9	3.81	33	205.2	179	104	136
Davis, Mark, S.F.*	5	17	5.36	46	174.2	201	54	124
Dawley, William, Hou.	11	4	1.93	60	98.0	82	35	47
Dedmon, Jeffrey, Atl.	4	3	3.78	54	81.0	86	35	51
DeLeon, Jose, Pitt	7	13	3.74	30	192.1	147	92	153
Denny, John, Phil.	7	7	2.45	22	154.1	122	29	94
DiPino, Frank, Hou.*	4	9	3.35	57	75.1	74	36	65
Dravecky, David, S.D.*	9	8	2.93	50	156.2	125	51	71
Eckersley, Dennis, Chi.	10	8	3.03	24	160.1	152	36	81
Falcone, Peter, Atl.*	5	7	4.13	35	120.0	115	57	55
Fernandez, C. Sid, N.Y.* ..	6	6	3.50	15	90.0	74	34	62
Franco, John, Cin.*	6	2	2.61	54	79.1	74	36	55
Frazier, George, Chi.	6	3	4.10	37	63.2	53	26	58
Gaff, Brent, N.Y.............	3	2	3.63	47	84.1	77	36	42
Garber, H. Eugene, Atl.....	3	6	3.06	62	106.0	103	24	55
Gooden, Dwight, N.Y.	17	9	2.60	31	218.0	161	73	276
Gossage, Richard, S.D.	10	6	2.90	62	102.1	75	36	84
Gross, Kevin, Phil..........	8	5	4.12	44	129.0	140	44	84

Pitcher and Club	W	L	ERA	G	IP	H	BB	SO
Gullickson, W., Mtl.	12	9	3.61	32	226.2	230	37	100
Hawkins, M.A., S.D.	8	9	4.68	36	146.0	143	72	77
Hershiser, Orel, L.A.	11	8	2.66	45	189.2	160	50	150
Holland, Alfred, Phil.*	5	10	3.39	68	98.1	82	30	61
Honeycutt, F., L.A.*	10	9	2.84	29	183.2	180	51	75
Hooton, Burt, L.A.	3	6	3.44	54	110.0	109	43	62
Horton, Ricky, St.L.*	9	4	3.44	37	125.2	140	39	76
Hudson, Charles, Phil.	9	11	4.04	30	173.2	181	52	94
Hume, Thomas, Cin.	4	13	5.64	54	113.1	142	41	59
James, Robert, Mtl.	6	6	3.66	62	96.0	92	45	91
Kepshire, Kurt, St.L.	6	5	3.30	17	109.0	100	44	71
Knepper, Robert, Hou.*	15	10	3.20	35	233.2	223	55	140
Koosman, Jerry, Phil.*	14	15	3.25	36	224.0	232	60	137
Krukow, Michael, S.F.	11	12	4.56	35	199.1	234	78	141
LaCoss, Michael, Hou.	7	5	4.02	39	132.0	132	55	86
Lahti, Jeffrey, St.L.	4	2	3.72	63	84.2	69	34	45
LaPoint, David, St.L.*	12	10	3.96	33	193.0	205	77	130
Laskey, William, S.F.	9	14	4.33	35	207.2	222	50	71
Lavelle, Gary, S.F.*	5	4	2.76	77	101.0	92	42	71
Lea, Charles, Mtl.	15	10	2.89	30	224.1	198	68	123
Lefferts, Craig, S.D.*	3	4	2.13	62	105.2	88	24	56
Lerch, Randy, S.F.*	5	3	4.23	37	72.1	80	36	48
Lollar, W.T., S.D.*	11	13	3.91	31	195.2	168	105	131
Lynch, Edward, N.Y.	9	8	4.50	40	124.0	169	24	62
Mahler, Richard, Atl.	13	10	3.12	38	222.0	209	62	106
McGaffigan, A., Mtl.-Cin.	3	6	3.52	30	69.0	60	23	57
McMurtry, J. Craig, Atl.	9	17	4.32	37	183.1	184	102	99
McWilliams, L., Pitt.*	12	11	2.93	34	227.1	226	78	149
Minton, Gregory, S.F.	4	9	3.76	74	124.1	130	57	48
Moore, Donnie, Atl.	4	5	2.94	47	64.1	63	18	47
Niekro, Joseph, Hou.	16	12	3.04	38	248.1	223	89	127
Orosco, Jesse, N.Y.*	10	6	2.59	60	87.0	58	34	85
Owchinko, R., Cin.*	3	5	4.12	49	94.0	91	39	60
Palmer, David, Mtl.	7	3	3.84	20	105.1	101	44	66
Pastore, Frank, Cin.	3	8	6.50	24	98.1	110	40	53
Pena, Alejandro, L.A.	12	6	2.48	28	199.1	186	46	135
Perez, Pascual, Atl.	14	8	3.74	30	211.2	208	51	145

Pitcher and Club	W	L	ERA	G	IP	H	BB	SO
Power, Ted, Cin.	9	7	2.82	78	108.2	93	46	81
Price, Joseph, Cin.*	7	13	4.19	30	171.2	176	61	129
Rainey, Charles, Chi........	5	7	4.28	17	88.1	102	38	45
Rawley, Shane, Phil.* 10		6	3.81	18	120.1	117	27	58
Reardon, Jeffrey, Mtl.	7	7	2.90	68	87.0	70	37	79
Reuschel, Ricky, Chi.	5	5	5.17	19	92.1	123	23	43
Reuss, Jerry, L.A.*	5	7	3.82	30	99.0	102	31	44
Rhoden, Richard, Pitt......14		9	2.72	33	238.1	216	62	136
Robinson, Don, Pitt.........	5	6	3.02	51	122.0	99	49	110
Robinson, Jeffrey, S.F......	7	15	4.56	34	171.2	195	52	102
Rogers, Stephen, Mtl......	6	15	4.31	31	169.1	171	78	64
Rucker, David, St.L.*......	2	3	2.10	50	73.0	62	34	38
Ruhle, Vernon, Hou.	1	9	4.58	40	90.1	112	29	60
Russell, Jeffrey, Cin........	6	18	4.26	33	181.2	186	65	101
Ruthven, Richard, Chi.	6	10	5.04	23	126.2	154	41	55
Ryan, L. Nolan, Hou. 12		11	3.04	30	183.2	143	69	197
Sanderson, Scott, Chi.	8	5	3.14	24	140.2	140	24	76
Schatzeder, D., Mtl.*	7	7	2.71	36	136.0	112	36	89
Scott, Michael, Hou........	5	11	4.68	31	154.0	179	43	83
Show, Eric, S.D..............15		9	3.40	32	206.2	175	88	104
Sisk, Douglas, N.Y.	1	3	2.09	50	77.2	57	54	32
Smith, Bryn, Mtl. 12		13	3.32	28	179.0	178	51	101
Smith, David, Hou.	5	4	2.21	53	77.1	60	20	45
Smith, Lee, Chi.............	9	7	3.65	69	101.0	98	35	86
Soto, Mario, Cin............18		7	3.53	33	237.1	181	87	185
Stoddard, T., Chi. 10		6	3.82	58	92.0	77	57	87
Stuper, John, St.L..........	3	5	5.28	15	61.1	73	20	19
Sutcliffe, Richard, Chi. 16		1	2.69	20	150.1	123	39	155
Sutter, H. Bruce, St.L......	5	7	1.54	71	122.2	109	23	77
Tekulve, Kenton, Pitt.......	3	9	2.66	72	88.0	86	33	36
Terrell, C. Walter, N.Y. 11		12	3.52	33	215.0	232	80	114
Thurmond, M., S.D.* 14		8	2.97	32	178.2	174	55	57
Tibbs, Jay, Cin.	6	2	2.86	14	100.2	87	33	40
Trout, Steven, Chi.*........13		7	3.41	32	190.0	205	59	81
Tudor, John, Pitt.* 12		11	3.27	32	212.0	200	56	117
Tunnell, B. Lee, Pitt........	1	7	5.27	26	68.1	81	40	51
Valenzuela, F., L.A.* 12		17	3.03	34	261.0	218	106	240

Pitcher and Club	W	L	ERA	G	IP	H	BB	SO
Welch, Robert, L.A.	13	13	3.78	31	178.2	191	58	126
Whitson, Eddie, S.D.	14	8	3.24	31	189.0	181	42	103
Williams, Frank, S.F.	9	4	3.55	61	106.1	88	51	91
Zachry, Patrick, L.A.	5	6	3.81	58	82.2	84	51	55

BRUCE WEBER PICKS
HOW THEY'LL FINISH IN 1985

American League East

1. Detroit
2. New York
3. Toronto
4. Boston
5. Baltimore
6. Milwaukee
7. Cleveland

American League West

1. Kansas City
2. Minnesota
3. Chicago
4. California
5. Seattle
6. Oakland
7. Texas

National League East

1. New York
2. Chicago
3. Philadelphia
4. St. Louis
5. Montreal
6. Pittsburgh

National League West

1. San Diego
2. Atlanta
3. Los Angeles
4. Houston
5. San Francisco
6. Cincinnati

American League Champions: Detroit
National League Champions: New York
World Champions: Detroit

YOU PICK
HOW THEY'LL FINISH IN 1985

**American League
East**

1.

2.

3.

4.

5.

6.

7.

**American League
West**

1.

2.

3.

4.

5.

6.

7.

**National League
East**

1.

2.

3.

4.

5.

6.

**National League
West**

1.

2.

3.

4.

5.

6.

American League Champions:

National League Champions:

World Champions: